SPIKE'S CHESS PRIMER

SPIKE'S CHESS PRIMER

GEORGE ELLISON

Illustrations by E.H.HANDFORTH

 THE CROWOOD PRESS

First published in 1983 by
The Crowood Press,
Ramsbury, Marlborough,
Wiltshire SN8 2HE

New edition 1988

British Library Cataloguing in Publication Data

Ellison, George
    Spike's Chess Primer
    1. Chess – Manuals – For children
    I. Title
    794.1'2

(First edition ISBN 0 946284 05 9 (HB))
                      0 946284 20 2 (PB))

ISBN 1 85223 157 2

Typeset by Andek, London
Printed in Great Britain by
Billing & Sons Ltd, Worcester

CONTENTS

Chapter 1

SPIKE INTRODUCES HIMSELF AND CHESS

Hi readers! My name is Spike and the unusual thing about me is that I carry a chessboard on my head!

"What a silly thing to do," you might say, but to me it seems the most natural thing.

You see, chess fascinates me. It is thrilling when you're winning, mind-boggling trying to think of the next move, and there's always a new idea to help you out of trouble . . . something that will make your opponent grit his teeth and make his skin go a sickly green colour.

If you think I'm the only one mad about chess then you're mistaken. Come with me to the Liverpool Junior Chess Congress held every Easter and I will show you over a thousand young chess players from five years old, happily sucking their ice lollies as they play, to rather serious adult-looking eighteen year olds.

All are so absorbed in their chess games that they won't even notice that you've arrived in the room.

Once one game is finished, another is started, then another and another and another.

Such is the fascination of chess that they don't stop for meals, preferring to bring their own sandwiches and pop to the board.

Do they grow out of this strange obsession? I'm pleased to say the answer is no. At adult chess clubs and congresses throughout the country you will find players from five to ninety years old, all equally batty about chess.

You are probably wondering who invented such an interesting game. Well, no one really knows. However, one legend is that when Agamemnon, the Greek leader, camped with his army outside Troy in an attempt to capture the city and the beautiful queen, Helen, his soldiers became bored and restless as month after month went by and the citizens of Troy refused to surrender. So Palamedes, one of his generals, had a brainwave and invented chess. The soldiers then played happily outside Troy for the next ten years and even managed to capture the city with the help of a wooden horse; but that's another story!

Far more likely, however, is that chess came from a board game for four players, called 'chaturanga', played with dice in India. About 1300 years ago the game changed into something like the game we play today; and it spread from India to Persia, Western Europe and, I'm glad to say, the British Isles.

WHAT IS CHESS?

Chess is an exciting game played by two players on a flat board with 64 squares. There are 32 white squares and 32 black squares. Here is the board, or the battlefield, ready for the beginning of the game.

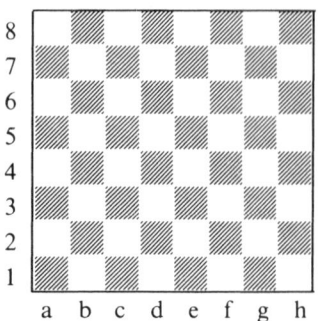

Notice that there is a white square in the right hand corner nearest each player.

The two players sit facing each other and each player has a set of pieces with which he or she tries to capture the other player's king.

Here is a way of showing the two armies facing each other at the beginning of the game.

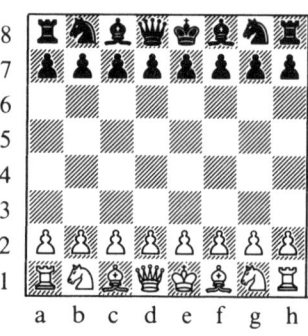

Each player moves in turn and White always starts the game.

You will be wondering what the pieces are called. Here are their names and the signs or symbols we use for each chess piece.

Names   Symbols

KING

QUEEN

ROOK

BISHOP

KNIGHT

PAWN

Each side has two rooks, two knights, two bishops, a king, a queen and eight pawns.

10

MORE ABOUT
THE CHESSBOARD

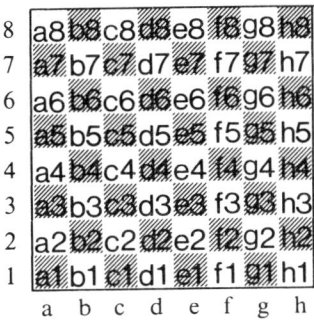

To make it easy to learn how to play chess you need to know the names of the squares.

Files

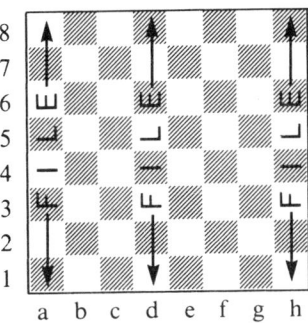

Each line of squares going from one player to the other is called a 'file'. The first file is called the 'a-file', the second the 'b-file', and so on. The arrows in the diagram are travelling along the a-file from a1 to a8, along the d-file from d1 to d8, and along the h-file from h1 to h8.

Remember that files are the lines of squares going up and down the board.

Ranks

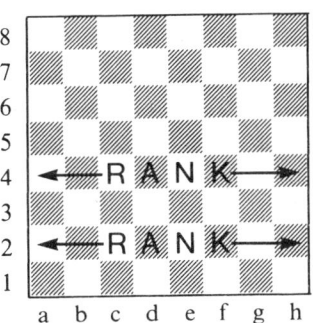

The lines of squares going across the board from left to right are called 'ranks'. In the diagram the arrows travel along the second rank from a2 to h2 and along the fourth rank from a4 to h4.

Diagonals

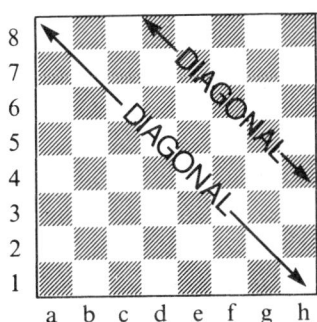

The lines of squares slanting across the board and cutting through the corners of the squares are called diagonals.

In the diagram the arrows go along the diagonal from h1 to a8 and from h4 to d8. Notice that a diagonal always has the *same* colour of square.

11

Exercise 1

(see answers in Chapter 22)

1. Place the board in the right position to begin the game.

2. Name the chess pieces.

3. Put the pieces on the board in the correct positions to begin the game.

4. Name the squares with a cross on them in the diagram.

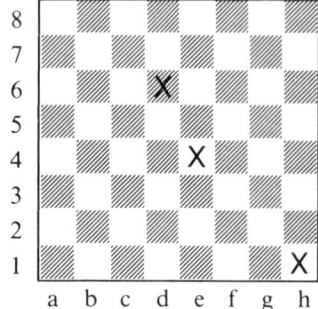

Chapter 2

THE ROOK OR CASTLE

In the earliest known form of chess all the pieces got their name from some part of the Indian army. The rook was a chariot that guarded the flanks of the advancing army and so had to be able to move about quickly to repel any sudden attack from the enemy. So in chess the rook was given a long move and made one of the strongest pieces.

When the game came to the West the rook became a castle, possibly because the lords and ladies who began to play chess liked to be reminded of their own great castles.

Just as the chariot had been important to the Indian army, so the castle was important to the great lord who owned it. It was also a place of safety in the event of attack by a foreign army. Indeed, if a castle fell then the war was often lost.

The castle in the game of chess can zoom up and down and across the board and is a good attacker like the chariot. Or, when placed in a good position, it can be a strong defence, like the castle of the middle ages.

HOW THE ROOK
OR CASTLE MOVES

From its own square the rook can go as far as it likes along the file a1 to a8 or the rank a1 to h1. It can stop at any point shown by the arrow.

Although the rook can move long distances speedily it can only do so if the way is clear. Should there be any of its own pieces or any enemy pieces in its path then it cannot move beyond them.

The rook on a1 cannot move forward because its own pawn is in the way and it cannot move to the side because its own knight blocks its path.

The rook takes by landing on the square where an enemy piece stands. The rook on a1 captures the knight on a6 and then remains on a6.

The rook in the diagram has captured the knight and now makes its next move from the square a6.

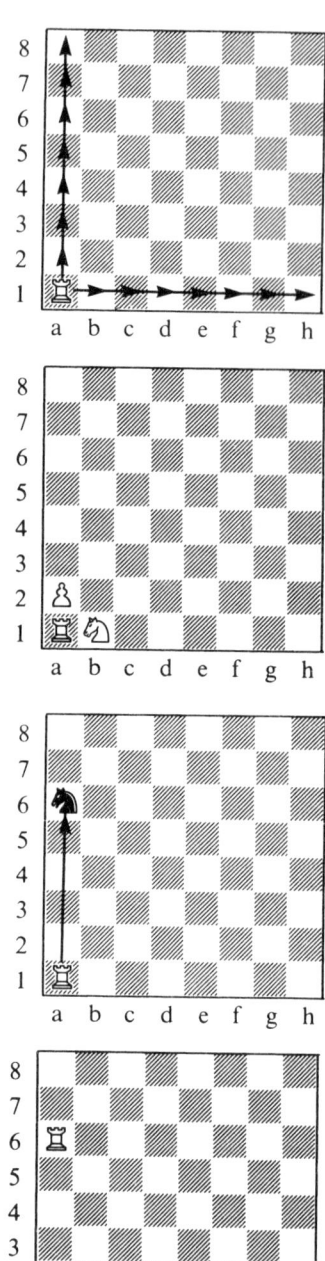

14

Rooks can move forwards, backwards or sideways.

A rook in the centre of the board can attack in four directions. A rook in the corner of the board can move in only two directions.

The rook on d5 in the diagram can take any of the four pieces, but of course it can only take any one piece in one move.

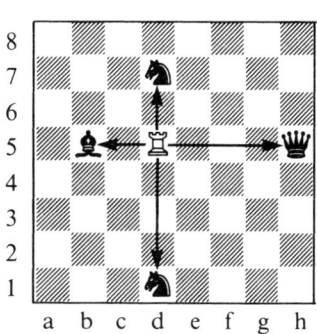

Exercise 2

(see answers in Chapter 22)

1. Which squares can the rook go to from b1?

2. Place a rook on e5 and then place four pieces on the board where they can be captured by the rook on its next move.

3. Look at the diagram and say which black piece the white rook cannot capture. Why not?

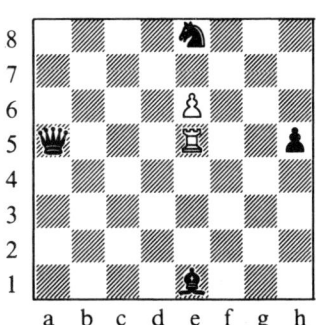

Chapter 3

THE KNIGHT

In olden days it was a mark of great honour to be made a knight. A boy would serve for years as squire to a knight and only if he proved to be patient, loyal and brave would he be made a knight himself. He attended to his master's needs and practised the arts of war, which included fencing, riding and using a lance and shield on horseback.

At a special ceremony called 'dubbing' a squire would be made a knight. An older knight would hand him a sword and give him a heavy blow with the flat of his hand on his face and neck. The new knight was then expected to leap onto his horse and charge with lance at a suit of armour to show what a good horseman he was.

Knights were expected to take part in tournaments in which each knight on horseback in full armour and carrying a lady's colours was expected to point his lance and charge at full speed at another knight and try to knock him off his horse. This was called jousting and knights were sometimes killed or badly injured.

Knights were expected to be loyal, brave and chivalrous. Bravery and loyalty to their king were shown by their willingness to fight for him in foreign wars. Chivalry was shown by helping the weak.

There are many stories of knights saving fair maidens in distress. Perhaps the most famous legend concerns Saint George fighting a fearsome dragon which was about to devour a young and beautiful princess. After a tremendous struggle in which St George was almost overcome by the smoke from the dragon's fire the noble knight summoned up all his strength and plunged his sword deep into the dragon's neck, killing it instantly.

Knights throughout the ages have fascinated people with their interesting adventures and so it is not surprising that they were chosen as pieces in the first Indian chess sets.

Because they spent so much time on horseback clearing obstacles the privilege of being the only piece able to jump over others was given to the chess knight by its inventor, and since the knight had to be nimble and quick to avoid blows on the battlefield he was also given the right to make the curious sideways move in chess.

Like the knights of old, learn to use the horse in your chess set well.

HOW THE KNIGHT MOVES

The knight moves either two squares forward and one square to the side or one square forward and two squares to the side.

In the diagram the knight on b1 can move to three squares: a3, c3 and d2. The arrows show the squares on which the knight can land.

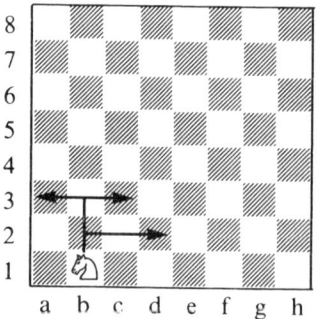

This diagram shows that the knight has moved from b1 to d2.

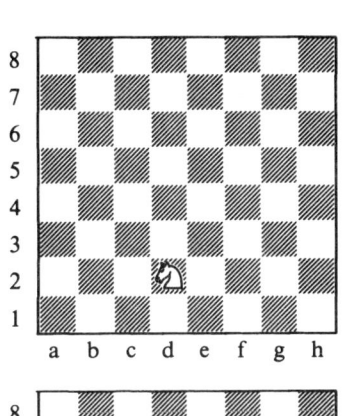

The knight can jump over other pieces just as a horse can jump over fences and obstacles. In the diagram the knight on g1 has jumped over two pawns to land on the square h3.

Here are two ways of remembering how the knight moves:

1. Think of the letter L when about to move your knight.
2. Think of two steps forward and one step to the side; or one step forward and two steps to the side.

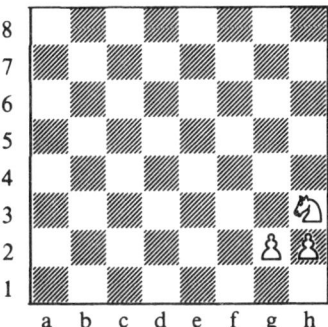

The knight on d5 can move to eight squares: b4, c3, e3, f4, b6, c7, e7 and f6.

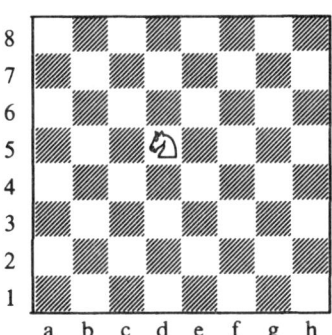

THE KNIGHT IN THE CENTRE OF THE BOARD

When the knight was on its starting square b1 it could only move to three squares. It is better placed in the centre where it can attack more pieces.

Here the knight on d4 can capture any one of the eight pieces on its next move.

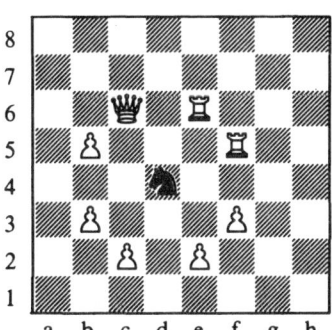

19

The knight on d4 has chosen to take the queen on c6.

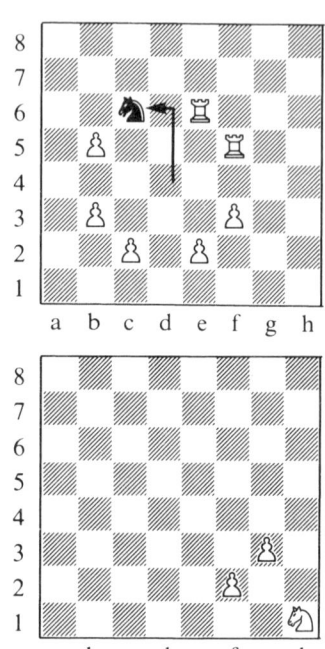

The knight on h1 in the diagram cannot move because the two squares, f2 and g3, on which it would normally land are occupied by pawns of the same colour.

Exercise 3

(see answers in Chapter 22)

1. Place pawns on squares to which a knight could move from g8.

2. Place pawns on squares to which a knight could move from e5.

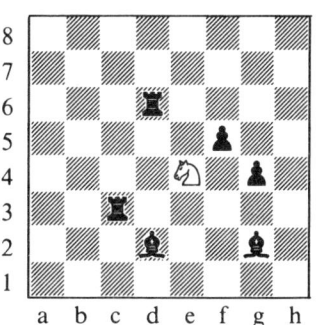

3. Which pieces can the knight on e4 capture? Say which squares they are on.

4. Now that you know the move of two chess pieces you can play a game of rooks and knights. You will enjoy it. Set up the board as in the diagram. There are just a few simple rules.

   a) White always moves first.

   b) If you touch a piece you must move it.

   c) The winner of the game is the first player to capture two of the other side's pieces.

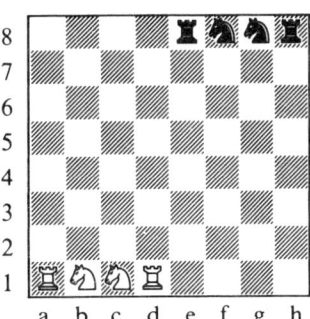

When you have played about a dozen games of rooks and knights you are ready to read on to the next chapter.

Chapter 4

THE QUEEN

In the first Indian chess sets there was no queen. The piece standing next to the king was called a counsellor or general and could only move one square diagonally at a time.

When chess came to Europe the queen replaced the counsellor and was given the right to move as far as she wanted to in any direction. Thus she became the most powerful piece on the board.

Perhaps the British queen most like the queen on the chessboard was Boadicea. She led her tribe into battle against the Romans. Attached to the wheels of her chariots were long knives which could cut off the Roman soldiers' legs. Indeed a whole Roman legion was destroyed in one battle against this fierce queen and her army.

Like Queen Boadicea, the queen on the chessboard is sharp and dangerous, often attacking several enemy pieces at the same time. No doubt the power of the queen as a chess piece pleased the ladies at court in the middle ages; by the same token it will probably please the girls who read this book.

THE QUEEN'S POSITION AT THE BEGINNING OF THE GAME

The white queen starts the game on the white square d1 and the black queen on the black square d8.

The diagram also shows that all the squares from the d-file to the a-file are called the *QUEENSIDE* of the board. These are a1-a8, b1-b8, c1-c8 and d1-d8.

All the squares from the e-file to the g-file are called the *KINGSIDE* of the board. These are e1-e8, f1-f8, g1-g8 and h1-h8.

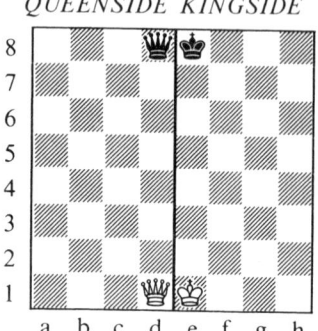

QUEENSIDE KINGSIDE

HOW THE QUEEN MOVES

The diagram shows that the queen can choose to move either like a rook or like a bishop.

The queen on d1 can go to any of the squares marked with an arrow. So, the queen can move five ways from d1: to the left or right along the rank a1 to h1; anywhere along the d-file; and along the two diagonals d1 to a4 and d1 to h5.

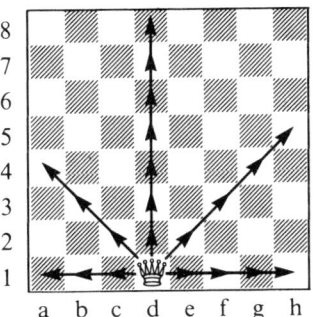

THE QUEEN IN THE CENTRE OF THE BOARD

As with all the other pieces, the queen is more powerful in the centre of the board than on the edge.

From the centre square d5 the queen can move in eight directions and land on twenty-seven different squares.

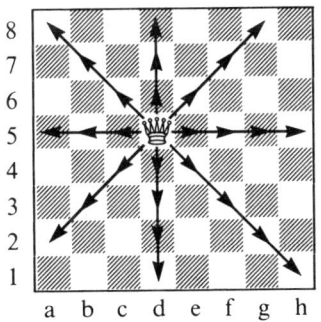

It can be seen that a queen has a great choice of where to move, so the player with a queen must look carefully to choose the best square to go to.

But the queen can only go to all the squares shown if there are no pieces or pawns blocking its path.

In the diagram the positions of the queen and the pieces around her are shown at the start of the game. You will see that the queen is surrounded by her own forces and cannot move anywhere! Unlike the knight, a queen cannot jump over other pieces.

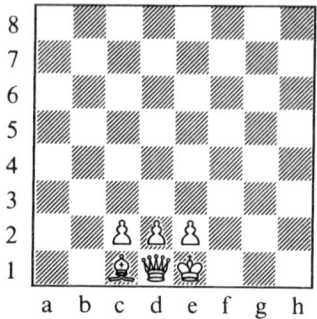

HOW THE QUEEN CAPTURES

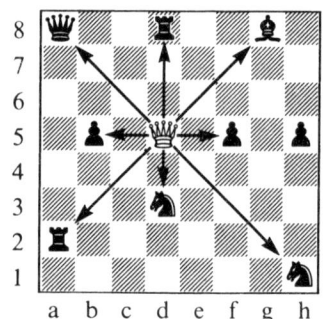

The queen captures by landing on a square where there is an enemy piece.

The queen can capture any of the pieces pointed to. It cannot take the pawn on h5 because the pawn on f5 is in the way.

Exercise 4

(see answers in Chapter 22)

1. Show all the moves of the queen from the squares (a) d8, and (b) e5.

2. Which pieces can the queen on f3 in the diagram capture?

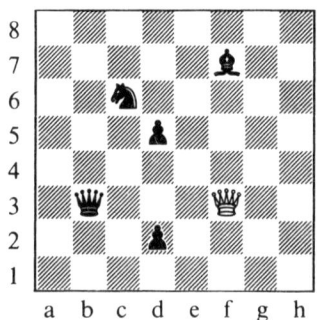

Chapter 5

THE BISHOP

In the first Indian chess sets one of the pieces was an elephant, a somewhat clumsy lumbering beast which usually moved slowly yet steadily on in the face of fierce opposition. So the inventor of chess only allowed it to move one or two squares along a diagonal in any one move.

When the game came to Europe, the elephant was replaced by the bishop. The bishop was an important figure in the church and at court in those times, and he probably came to mind when the leading chess players of the time were looking for a new piece. The bishop was able to move far faster than the elephant, in fact to any square he wanted to go to along a diagonal. This speeded up the game considerably and made it far more enjoyable.

In the middle ages some bishops were known to be scheming and sly; maybe this is why he was given the diagonal move in chess . . . slanting across the board!

HOW THE BISHOP MOVES

Each player has two bishops, one on the c-file and the other on the f-file.

A bishop always moves on the same colour of square as it begins the game on. In the diagram the bishop on f1 can move to any of the squares marked with an arrow. It moves diagonally, cutting through the corners of the squares in a slanting way. So the bishop on f1 can move to e2, d3, c4, b5 and a6, and to g2 and h3.

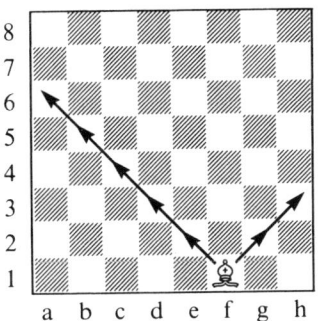

White's other bishop, which starts the game on c1, will always move on the black squares.

THE BISHOP IN THE CENTRE OF THE BOARD

In the diagram the white-squared bishop in the centre of the board can move to any of the squares marked with an arrow along the diagonals a2 to g8 and h1 to a8.

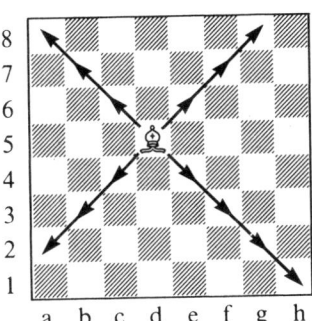

It is better placed in the centre of the board than on its starting square. The bishop in the centre on d5 can go to thirteen squares. Compare this with the bishop on f1 which could only travel to seven squares. So, a bishop in the centre is almost twice as powerful as a bishop on the edge of the board.

A bishop cannot jump over its own pieces or pawns. The bishop on f1 in the diagram cannot move because there are pawns on e2 and g2.

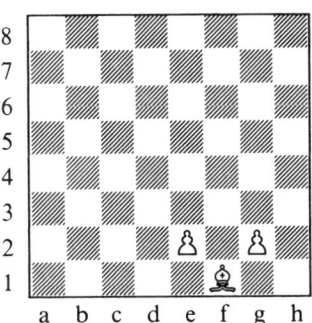

So, in order to give the bishop room to move you should move at least one of the blocking pawns early in the game.

29

HOW THE BISHOP CAPTURES

A bishop captures by landing on the square on which an enemy piece is standing.

In the diagram the bishop on e6 can take any one of the four pieces shown.

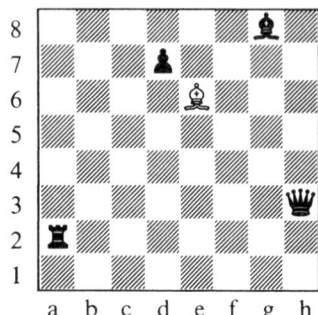

The bishop has captured the rook by landing on the square a2. The bishop will now stay on a2 until it makes another move.

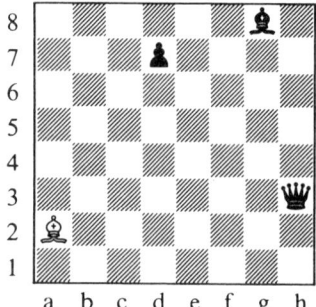

A bishop cannot jump over enemy pieces or pawns.

The bishop on d5 in the diagram cannot capture the enemy queen on a2 because there is an enemy pawn in the way on b3; but it could capture the pawn on b3 and threaten to capture the queen on its next move.

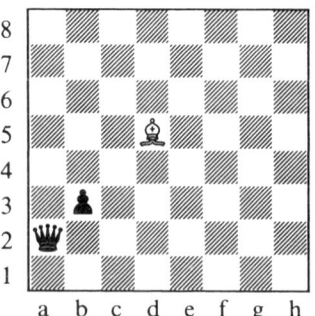

Exercise 5

(see answers in Chapter 22)

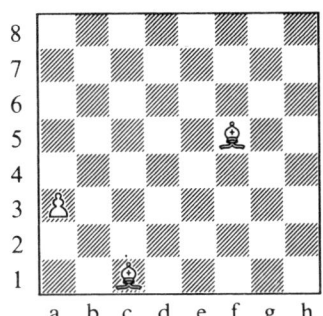

1. To which squares can the bishop on c1 move?

2. To which squares can the bishop on f5 move?

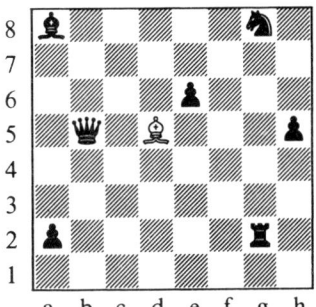

3. Which pieces can the bishop on d5 capture?

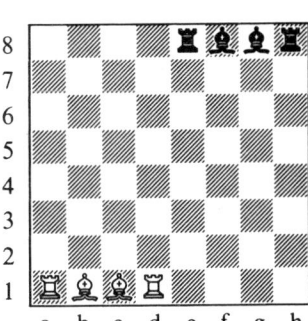

Now that you know the bishop's moves you can play the game of rooks and bishops.

Set up the board as in the diagram.

The rules are the same as for rooks and knights. Remember that the first player to capture two enemy pieces has won the game.

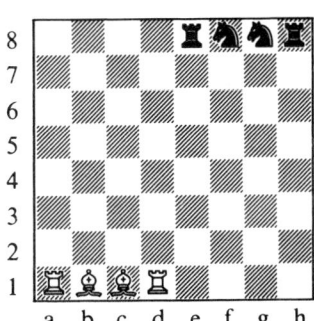

You can also play rooks and bishops against rooks and knights. Rules as before, but set up the board as in this diagram.

Chapter 6

THE KING

In days of old the king was very important. If he was captured or killed in battle his troops would surrender or flee the field of battle, and the other side would claim victory. At the Battle of Hastings in 1066 AD King Harold of England was killed by an arrow piercing his eye. Immediately his Saxon army ran away and the Normans won the battle.

So it is in chess also – if the king is captured, the game is lost. Although the king is the most important piece on the chessboard he is only allowed to move one square at a time. Perhaps this is to discourage him from placing himself in danger.

HOW THE KING MOVES

The king's moves are very easy to learn. He can move just one square in any direction.

The king on e1 in the diagram can move to all the squares shown by the arrows: d1, d2, e2, f2 and f1.

THE KING IN THE CENTRE OF THE BOARD

If the king is in the centre of the board he can move to more squares than when he is on the side. The king on d5 in the diagram can go to the eight squares shown by the arrows. The king on e1 could only go to five squares.

A king cannot move onto a square on which one of his own pieces stands. So at the beginning of the game the king cannot move. The king on e1 is surrounded by his own men on d1, d2, e2, f2 and f1.

Exercise 6

(see answers in Chapter 22)

To which squares can a king on c6 move?

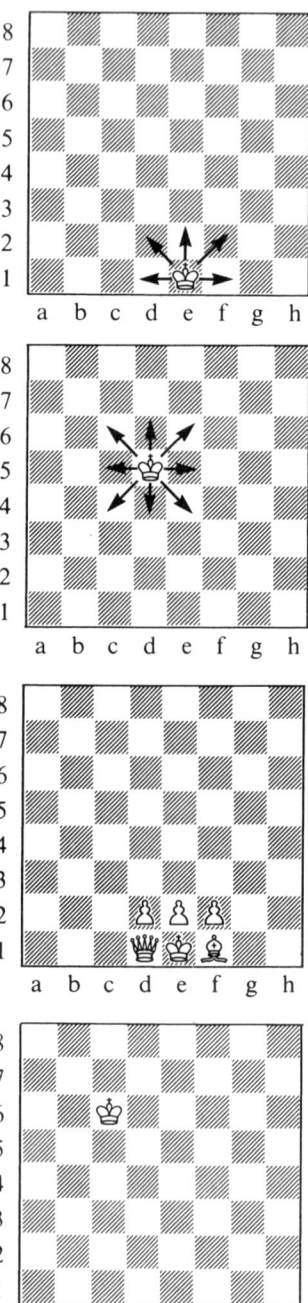

Chapter 7

THE PAWNS

Every army has ordinary foot soldiers and in the British army they are called infantry. In chess the foot soldiers are called pawns. At the beginning of the game a pawn stands in front of each piece to protect it. Because the pawns are at the front of each army they face the greatest danger of capture.

At first you might say "Well, it doesn't matter if I lose a few pawns – I have eight!". But when you have played some games you will find out that the pawns are important and should be looked after. This is because each pawn can become a queen, or any piece except for a king, if it can reach the far end of the board. In order to do this it has to pass the enemy pawns facing it and to survive attacks from the enemy pieces; so it really does deserve promotion if it can make it to the other end!

Good generals always look after their foot soldiers. You, as general of your chess army, must look after your pawns.

HOW PAWNS MOVE

Pawns can only move forwards and so are different from all the other pieces, which can go either forwards or backwards.

35

On its first move a pawn can move either one square forward or two squares forward.

The pawn on b2 moves one square forward to b3. The pawn on d2 moves two squares forwards to d4.

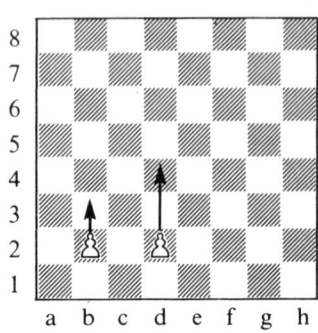

This diagram shows the position of the two pawns when they have moved.

After its first move a pawn can only advance one square each move. So the pawn on b3 in the diagram can only move to b4 on its next move, and the pawn on d4 to d5.

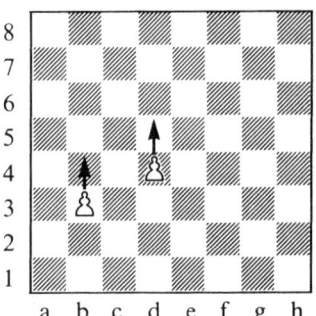

If one of its own pieces or an enemy piece is on the square in front of a pawn, then the pawn cannot move.

The pawn on c4 in the diagram cannot move forward because its own king is blocking the way to c5. The pawn on f5 cannot move because the enemy knight is on the square in front of the pawn.

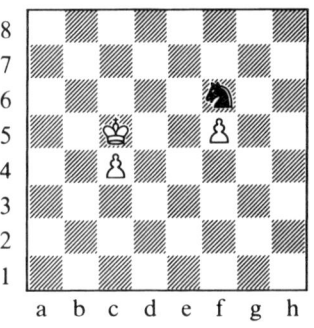

HOW PAWNS CAPTURE

Pawns cannot capture enemy pieces on the file on which they stand. The knight on f6 in the last diagram is safe from capture by the pawn on f5.

36

Pawns capture by taking diagonally one square forward.

In the diagram the white pawn on c4 can capture either the rook on d5 or the pawn on b5.

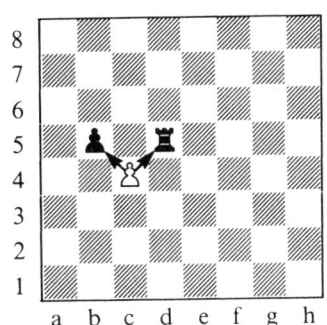

The pawn has captured the enemy pawn on b5 by landing on the square on which it stood.

It will now carry on moving forwards one square at a time along the b-file.

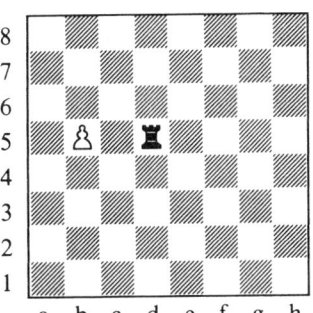

When a pawn reaches the other end of the board it becomes a queen or any other piece you choose, apart from a king.

The pawn on f7 in the diagram moves forward to become a queen upon reaching f8. All you do is pick up the pawn on f8 and replace it with whatever piece you choose – normally a queen.

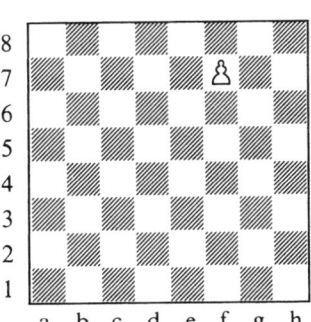

It is possible for a player to have nine queens; but in practice it rarely happens that a player has more than three queens on the board at any one time.

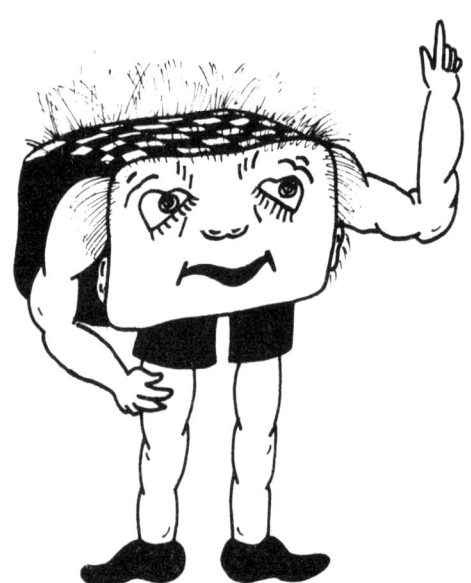

A NOTE ON *EN PASSANT*

There's one more thing to know about how pawns capture. This is a rather special rule, called *en passant*, which comes into effect occasionally.

Suppose that you have a pawn on the fifth rank and your opponent has a pawn on the next file on the seventh rank (see diagram 1). Then if he plays his pawn up two squares, so that it is next to yours (see diagram 2) you can capture it as if he had only moved it one square. The position after the capture is shown in diagram 3.

There are two points to remember about this rule: you can only capture this way on the move immediately after your opponent moves his pawn, and you can only do this sort of capture with pawns, not with other pieces.

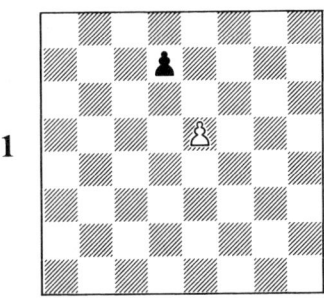

1

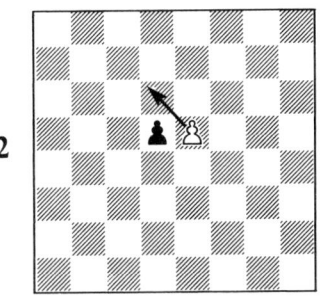

2

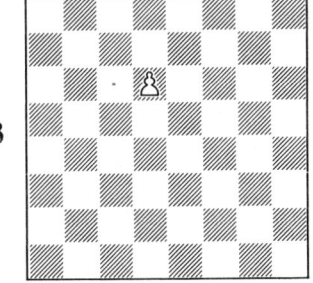

3

Exercise 7

(see answers in Chapter 22)

Look at the diagram and answer the questions.

1. Which pawns can move without capturing?

2. To which squares can they move?

3. Which pawn can capture an enemy piece?

4. Which square will it capture on?

5. Which white pawn cannot move?

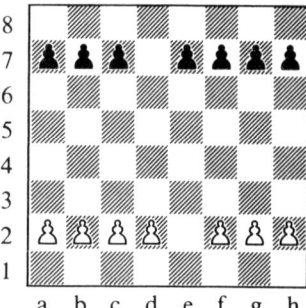

Why not try a few pawn games?

(a) Often in a grandmaster game of chess one player has four pawns on the king's side of the board and his opponent has three pawns there. On the queenside his opponent has four pawns and our player has only three. The game is often won by the player who can queen a pawn first. So it is a good idea to practise playing a game with pawns in which the winner is the player to queen a pawn first. Set up the position in the diagram and play a few games in which the winner is the first player to queen a pawn.

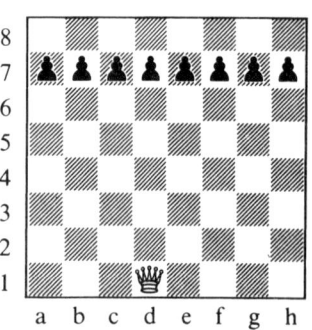

(b) Another interesting game is queen against pawns. Set up the position in the diagram and play a game in which the winner is either the player with the queen who has captured all eight pawns before they reach the other end of the board or the player with the pawns who manages

40

to reach the other end with one pawn (if one pawn gets through to the eighth rank then the player with the pawns is the winner). This game is like a game of British Bulldog – ask your teacher how to play! The player with the pawns has first move.

(c) Add a king to both sides. The winner is still the player either to capture the pawns or make a queen with one of the pawns. The starting position is shown in the diagram.

In this game the queen can capture the king. If the king is threatened with capture it must try to avoid being taken.

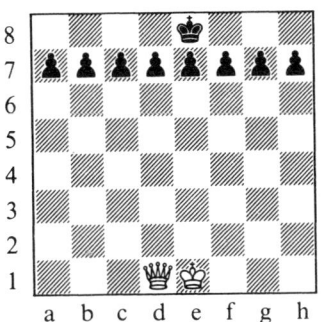

You now know a number of interesting games which can be played with chess pieces; and if you have followed the suggested exercises so far, you will have practised moving all the pieces. This is a good start to learning to play a full game of chess.

Chapter 8

CHECK

If the king is attacked by an enemy piece and could be captured on the next move then it is in **check**. The player attacking the king may warn his opponent by saying "check" and the player in check must try to get out of check.

In the diagram the black pawn on f5 is threatening to capture the white king on e4, so the white king is in check. What can he do?

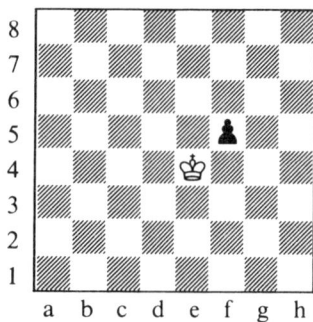

He can capture the piece giving check

The king has captured the pawn and so is no longer in check.

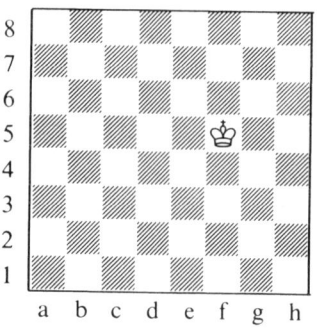

He can move out of check

The white king has moved from e4 to f4 and is no longer threatened with capture.

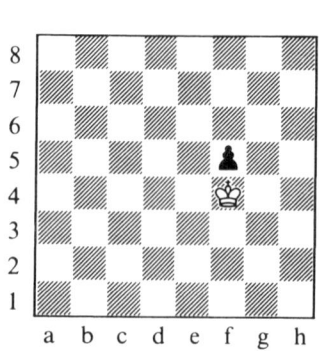

In the diagram the white queen on a2 is checking the black king on f7. Black plays his bishop to e6, placing it between the checking queen and the threatened king.

In cases where the king is in check from a piece more than one square away, it may often be possible for the defending side to place one of his own pieces between his king and the piece giving check. This is called **interposing** a piece.

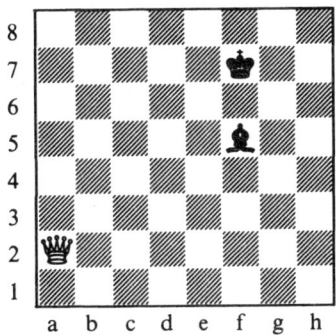

This is the position after Black's move. The white queen's attack on the black king has been blocked by the bishop. In fact, to avoid capture herself the white queen must now move away from the a2-g8 diagonal.

So, there are three ways of avoiding check:

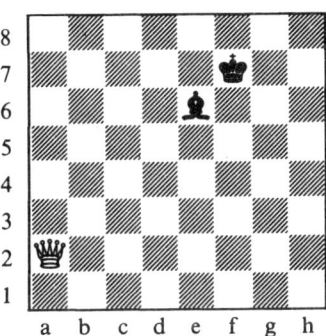

1. By moving your king out of range of the checking piece.

2. By capturing the checking piece.

3. By interposing a piece.

Exercise 8

(see answers in Chapter 22)

1. In this position the black pawn is checking the king. Find two ways of avoiding check.

2. In this position the black knight is checking the king. Find two ways of avoiding check.

3. In this position the black bishop is checking the king. Find three ways of avoiding check.

4. In this position the black rook is checking the king. Find three ways of avoiding check.

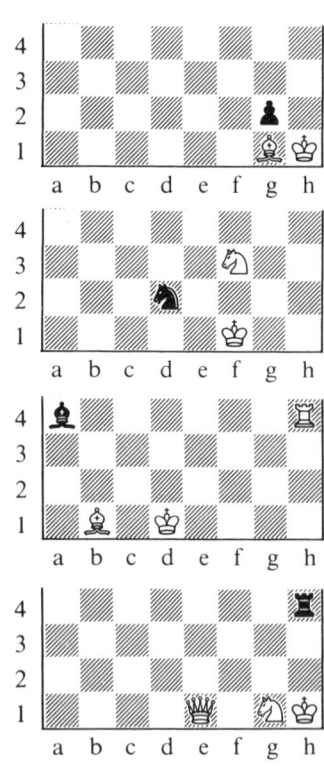

Chapter 9

CHECKMATE

The invading army had stormed the palace, but Ludwig thought that he might still escape because the enemy were still three rooms away.

"The secret passageway to the stables will take me to my trusty steed, Jason", he thought. "I will then be carried safely across the border."

Ludwig locked the door of his room, opened the window and slid down the drainpipe to the courtyard below.

As he landed on the cobbles he could hear the enemy above beating on the door he had just locked. "I must be quick", he said to himself.

Ludwig then dashed across the old courtyard and pushed hard against the secret panel that led to the secret passageway. The door slowly creaked open on rusty hinges and Ludwig disappeared inside. Soon he was at the end of the passageway and beneath the trap-door.

"I am within a whisker of freedom", he speculated. He then pushed open the old trap and climbed up into the stables above.

"Surrender", cried some voices, "Surrender or you die." Ludwig looked up. There were three of the enemy staring down at him. He had been betrayed.

In chess, when the king is threatened and cannot avoid capture, he is said to be 'checkmated'. The side whose king is checkmated loses the game. In the story King Ludwig had no escape and had to surrender.

The black king in the diagram is unable to move to a square that is not attacked by the white rook. There is no escape for him either. It is checkmate.

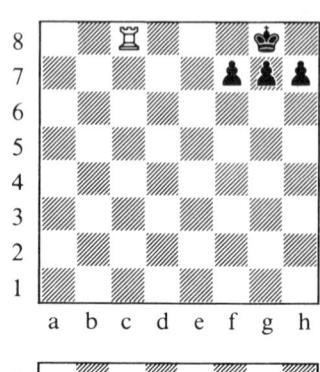

Here the black knight is checking the white king. White's own pieces are in the way and there is nowhere to go.

This checkmate is called 'smothered mate' because the king is smothered by his own pieces.

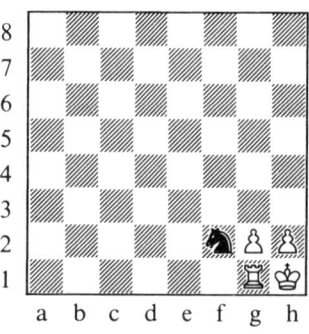

The white bishop is checking the black king. It is checkmate because the king cannot move to a square that is not attacked by the enemy bishop.

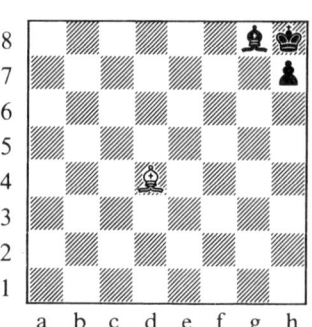

In this diagram the white queen has checkmated the black king. The black king cannot capture the white queen because a king cannot move onto a square next to another king, since the other king could then capture it on his move.

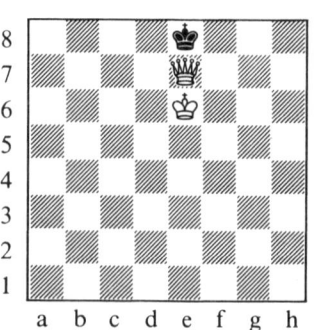

Here the black pawn on g2 is checking the white king on h1. Is it checkmate? Yes, because the king cannot take the pawn on g2 as it would then be taken by the pawn on h3.

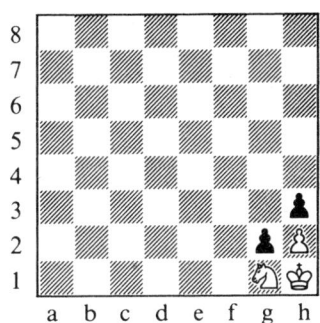

If you manage to checkmate your opponent's king you have won the game even if he has far more pieces than you have. In the diagram Black has only a knight and a king left against a powerful army, but it is Black who has won the game as there is no way for White to escape from the smothered mate. White has been very careless to allow Black's only piece to checkmate him. White has been thinking only of what he can do and has forgotten that his opponent can checkmate too.

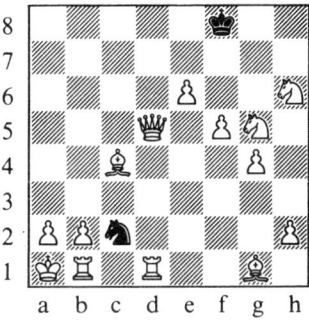

From the examples given you might get the idea that checkmate always happens when there are just a few pieces left on the board. This often happens, but now and then checkmate takes place very near to the start of a game. Here are three well known positions where this happens.

After only two moves the black queen has checkmated the white king. This mate is called 'fool's mate' because White has played very foolishly by moving both these pawns.

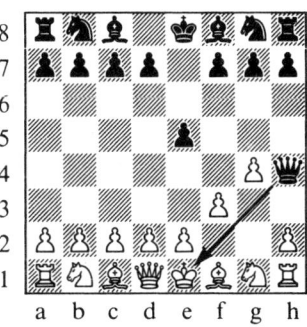

47

Here White has checkmated Black after only four moves by using his bishop and his queen to attack Black's king. Notice that the king cannot capture the queen because the bishop on c4 would then capture the king on f7 next move. This checkmate is called 'scholar's mate'.

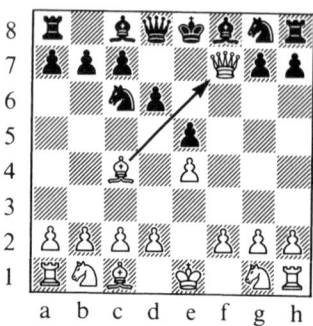

This position is astonishing. Black has won White's queen but is mated by the two knights and bishop. This shows how powerful two knights can be which are well placed in the centre of the board. This checkmate was first played by a Frenchman named Légal and is called 'Légal's mate'.

Exercise 9

(see answers in Chapter 22)

Which of these positions is checkmate? Some positions are not checkmate. Say why they are not checkmate.

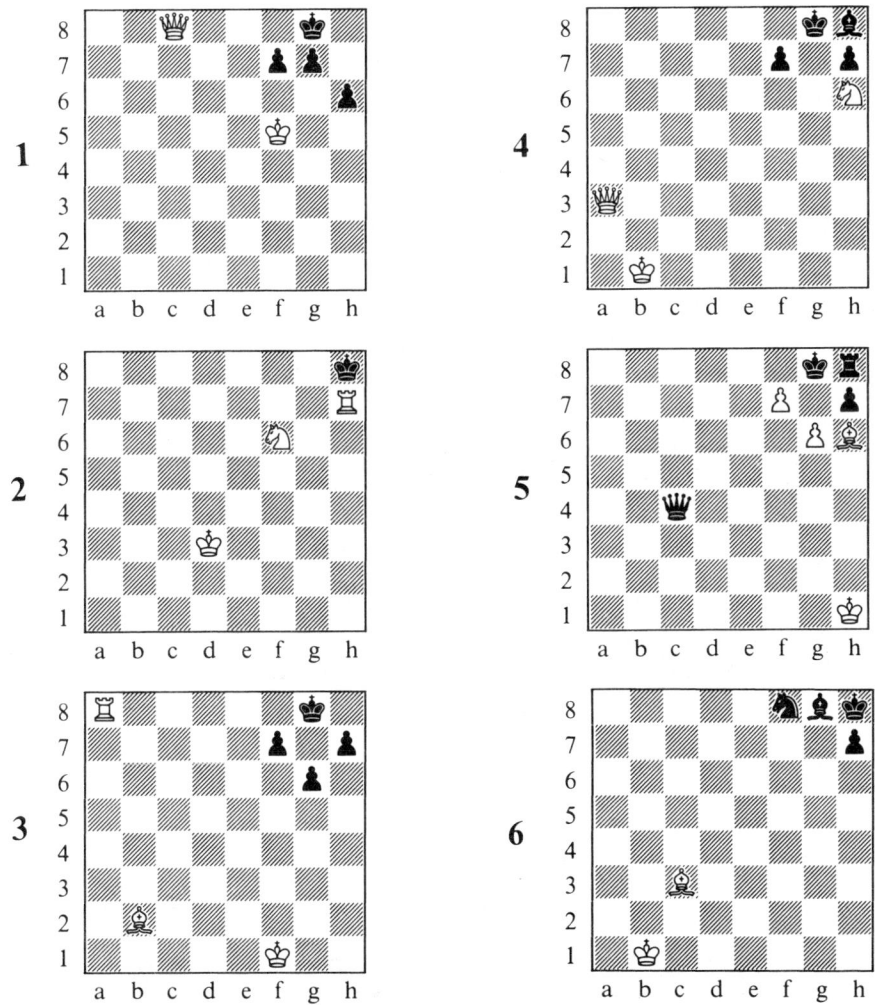

Chapter 10

CASTLING

I'm now going to teach you a new and unusual move called 'castling'.

In the old Indian game of chess the king could only plod to the safety of a corner of the board by making one move at a time.

When the game came to the West players found this way rather slow and so brought in a new move called castling which speeded up the action considerably.

When castling you are allowed to move the king and the rook at the same time, provided that neither of them have been moved already.

HOW TO CASTLE

In **one** move the king moves from e1 to g1 and the rook from h1 to f1.

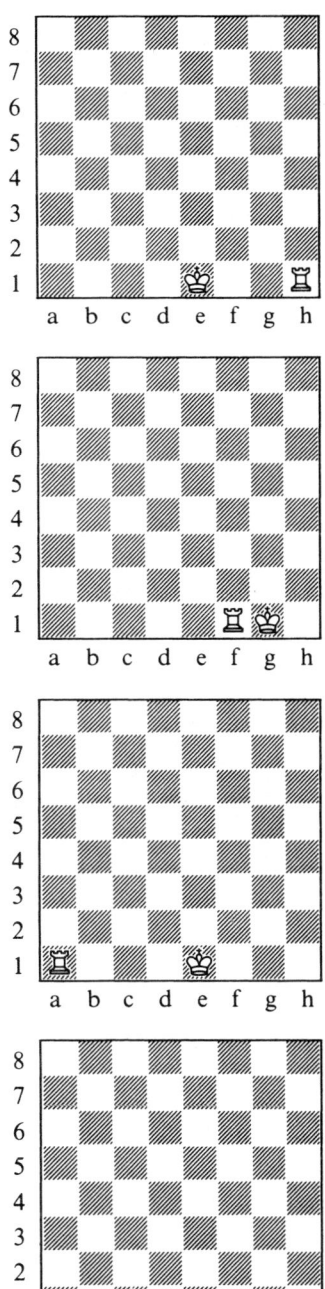

Here is the position after castling.

This movement is called 'kingside castling'. After castling on the kingside there is one empty square, h1, next to the king.

Castling on the queenside is a little different.

In one move the king moves from e1 to c1 and the rook from a1 to d1. So the rook on a1 has moved three squares to the right.

After queenside castling there are two empty squares, a1 and b1, next to the king.

51

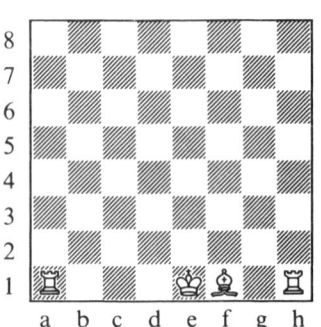

WHEN CAN'T YOU CASTLE?

1.   If one of your own pieces or an enemy piece stands on the rank between the king and the rook you cannot castle

In the diagram White cannot castle on the kingside because his bishop is in the way, but there is nothing to stop him from castling on the queenside.

2. Once you have moved your king, on e1 or e8, to another square, you cannot castle, even if you move it back to e1 or e8.

3. You cannot castle if you are in check.

4. You cannot castle if either the square the king is going to or the square across which the king has to travel in order to get to it is attacked by an enemy piece.

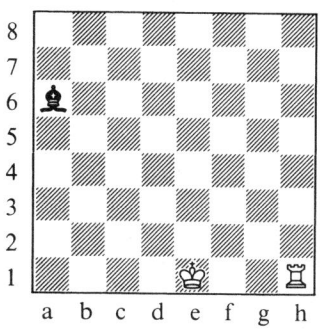

In the diagram the bishop on a6 is attacking the square f1, so White cannot castle on the kingside.

If later in the game White places a piece between the bishop attacking f1 and f1 itself he can then castle.

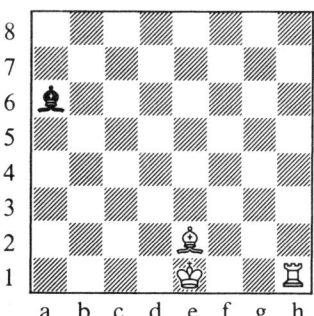

In the diagram White can now castle because his bishop on e2 stops the black bishop's attack on f1.

5. If a rook has already been moved you cannot castle on that side of the board.

For example, if the queen's rook has been moved to b1 then queenside castling is impossible, even if afterwards the rook on b1 is moved to its starting square, a1, although it might still be possible to castle on the kingside.

HOW TO CASTLE

You must **FIRST** pick up **YOUR KING** and place it on the square it is going to when castled, and then move the rook to its new square. If you pick up the rook first, your opponent can claim that you intended to move only the rook and he can stop you from castling. This has happened in both local league and tournament play.

IS CASTLING A GOOD IDEA?

If we look at the games of the top players in the world, called grandmasters, we find that they often castle at a fairly early stage of the game. They do so to get their king to a safer square and to place their rook onto a square nearer the centre of the board. You will remember that rooks, like other pieces, are more powerful in the centre. Tucked away in their own corner, they can often do very little to influence the course of the game.

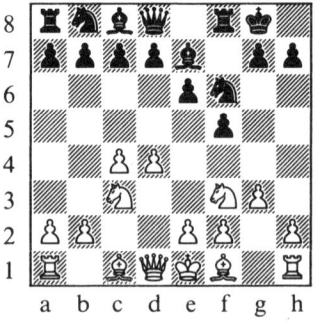

So, castling is a good idea, because it helps the king to safety and brings the rook into play in a single manoeuvre.

The diagram shows a position reached by the former World Champion Mikhail Tal.

After only five moves of the game Tal, playing Black, has castled. His rook on f8 is now nicely placed to attack the white king along the f-file, and his king is tucked safely away.

So, like Mikhail Tal, castle early in your games!

54

Exercise 10

(see answers in Chapter 22)

In which of the next six positions can Black castle?

If he cannot castle, say why.

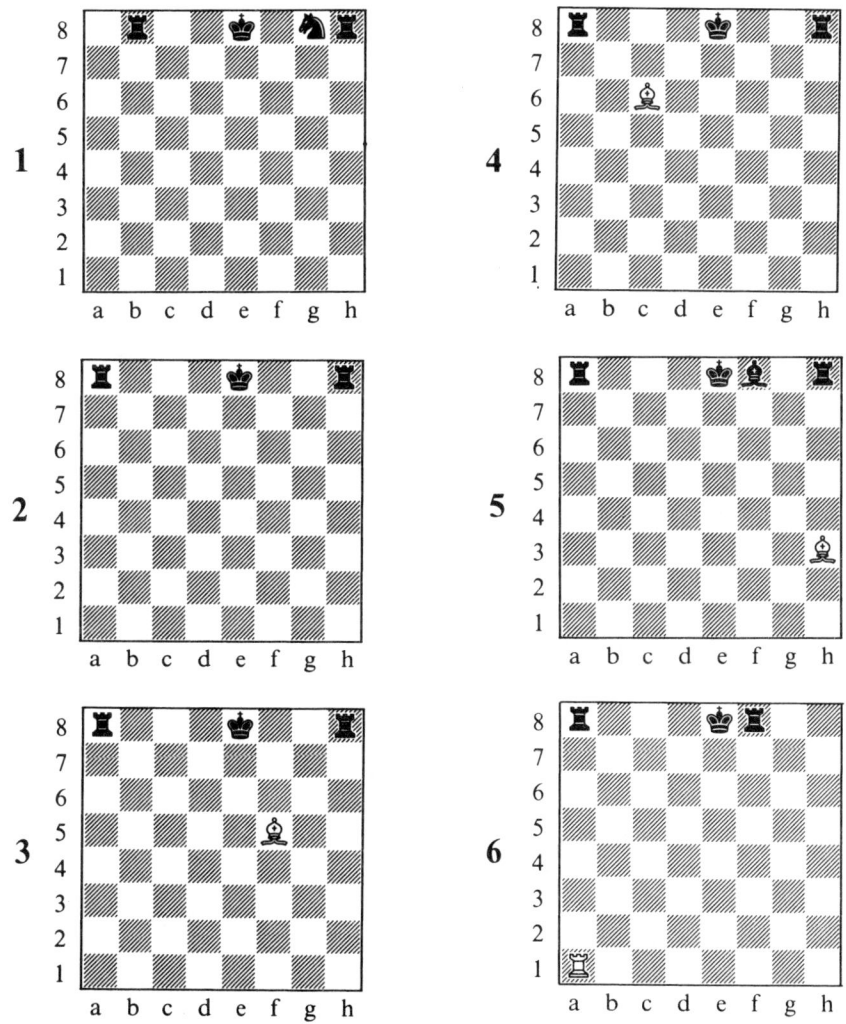

Chapter 11

WRITING DOWN YOUR GAME

When I started to play chess I enjoyed it so much that I didn't want anything to interfere with my game.

I couldn't understand why good players always wrote down their moves. Why did they waste time?

I talked it over with them, and they gave me several good reasons.

If you play a very good game, you are pleased with it and want to show your friends. There is nothing more annoying than wanting to show the game but finding out that you have forgotten some of the moves. You say, "I think he did this . . . no, it was that . . . sorry, he moved his queen." Your friends are bored and don't want to know.

If you write the moves down you can read them from your scoresheet and there is no danger of forgetting. With your scoresheet at hand you can go over the game with your friends or your opponent and find better moves for both sides. All of the top players do this, usually just after the end of the game. They jokingly call it the 'post mortem', as they want to find out why one king has died.

There is no better way of improving your game than going over it in this way. If you lose you can show your opponent that he was lucky and was really losing right throughout the game!

Finally, if you can write down your own games then you can read the games of other players. A very good way to improve is to read chess books with games and positions of good players. In Chapter 21 there is a list of books which are well worth reading.

HOW TO WRITE DOWN OR RECORD YOUR GAME

As you already know the names of all the squares you have a flying start in learning to record your games.

All you need to learn are the letters given to each of the pieces. These are:

R for **rook**

N for **knight**

B for **bishop**

K for **king**

Q for **queen**

Let's record a short game to show how it is done. Take a biro or pencil and a piece of paper. At the top of your paper write the names of the two players, one on the left hand side of the page, and the other on the right hand side. Like this:

White	*Black*
Fred Smith	**Joe Bloggs**

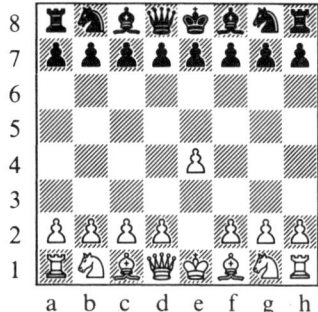

Now look at the position on the board in the diagram.

White, playing up the board, has moved the pawn in front of his king two squares forward to e4. When a pawn moves we just write down the square it lands on – like this:

White	*Black*
Fred Smith	**Joe Bloggs**
1 e4	

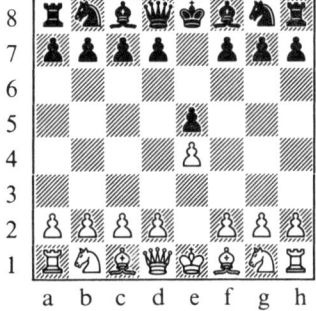

It is now **Joe Bloggs'** turn to move. He plays the pawn in front of his king forward two squares to e5.

The scoresheet now shows

White	*Black*
Fred Smith	**Joe Bloggs**
1 e4	**e5**

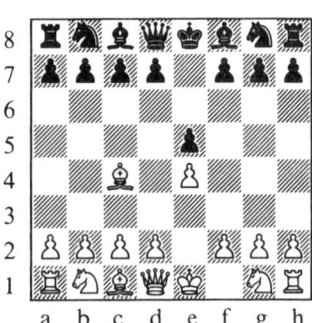

White now plays his bishop on f1 to c4, so the position now looks like this

and under **Fred Smith** we now write **2 Bc4**.

The score now reads

White	Black
White	*Black*
Fred Smith	**Joe Bloggs**
1 e4	e5
2 Bc4	

Black now moves his knight on b8 to c6. The position on the board looks like this

and under **Joe Bloggs** we write **2 ... Nc6**.

White	*Black*
Fred Smith	**Joe Bloggs**
1 e4	e5
2 Bc4	Nc6

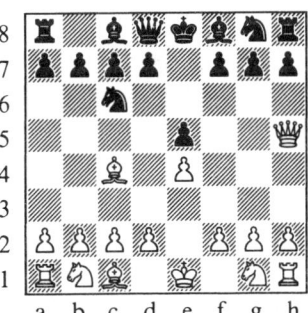

Fred Smith now plays his queen from d1 to h5. The position looks like this

and under **Fred Smith** we write **3 Qh5**.

The score now looks like this.

White	*Black*
Fred Smith	**Joe Bloggs**
1 e4	e5
2 Bc4	Nc6
3 Qh5	

Joe Bloggs now plays his pawn on a7 to a6, so we write **3 ... a6**.

The score now reads

White	*Black*
Fred Smith	**Joe Bloggs**
1 e4	e5
2 Bc4	Nc6
3 Qh5	a6

You should have been there to see the look on Joe Bloggs' face when Fred Smith moved his queen from h5 and took the pawn on f7 and said in a very loud voice which everyone in the room could hear **'CHECKMATE'**.

Joe couldn't believe it at first. Surely he couldn't have lost so quickly. But here it is.

THE FINAL POSITION

The scoresheet now looks like this.

	White	Black
	White	*Black*
	Fred Smith	**Joe Bloggs**
1	e4	e5
2	Bc4	Nc6
3	Qh5	a6
4	**Qf7 checkmate**	

There is just one more thing to learn about keeping your score. When you castle on the kingside you write **O-O**. When you castle on the queenside you write **O-O-O**.

Now that you know how to score, try writing down your games. You'll find it pays.

WHAT ARE THE PIECES WORTH?

Often during a game there is the chance to swap one piece for another. So it is useful to know what the pieces are worth.

Here is a table showing how many points each piece is worth.

♕ ♛	=	9 points
♖ ♜	=	5 points
♗ ♝	=	3 points
♘ ♞	=	3 points
♙ ♟	=	1 point

Using this table we can work out that

$$\text{♛} + \text{♙} \qquad = \text{♖} + \text{♖}$$

$$\text{♛} \qquad\qquad = \text{♗} + \text{♗} + \text{♘}$$

$$\text{♛} \qquad\qquad = \text{♘} + \text{♘} + \text{♗}$$

$$\text{♗} \qquad\qquad = \text{♘}$$

$$\text{♗} + \text{♙} + \text{♙} = \text{♖}$$

$$\text{♘} + \text{♙} + \text{♙} = \text{♖}$$

This is a very useful table but it is only meant to be used as a guide to what to do. Sometimes the position on the board makes the pieces worth far more or less than the number of points given in the table.

Look at this diagram, taken from a game played by grandmaster Hort.

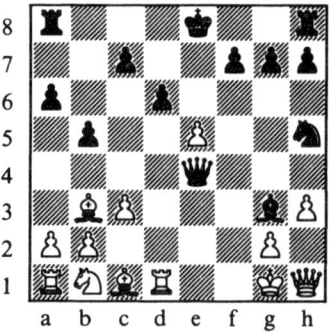

If we count the pieces we find that Black is a bishop down, so he is three points behind. But if we take a careful look at the position of the pieces we find that White's queen on h1 has no way of getting out of the corner without being captured and is therefore worth far less than Black's bishop on g3.

Compare the terrible position of White's queen with the magnificent position of Black's queen on e4, free to move to any part of the board. Hort, playing Black, quickly won this game.

It is not always the side with most points who wins the game. The position of the pieces must also be taken into consideration.

Exercise 11

(see answers in Chapter 22)

Play through the game given below and see if you can reach the correct position.

	WHITE	BLACK
1.	e4	c6
2.	d4	d5
3.	f3	de4
4.	Nc3	ef3
5.	Nf3	Bg4
6.	Bc4	Bf3
7.	Qf3	Nf6
8.	Be3	e6
9.	O-O	Nb8d7*
10.	Ne4	Be7
11.	Ng5	Nf8
12.	g4	h6
13.	Qh3	Ng6
14.	Nf7	Kf7
15.	g5	Qd7
16.	gf6	Bf6
17.	Qh5	Resigns

Black resigned as there is no way to avoid the loss of a piece by 18. Bd3.

* *As both the knight on f6 and the knight on b8 can go to d7 it is necessary to write* **Nb8d7**.

Chapter 12

KING AND QUEEN AGAINST KING

Ten year old Ahmed Patel had only been playing chess for just over a month when, to his surprise and pleasure, he was asked to play for the Northcliffe Junior team against Ashley, another local school. When he told his father that he had been selected, he said, "You must play with great care and make sure that you win."

So Ahmed, although very nervous, was determined to try his very best.

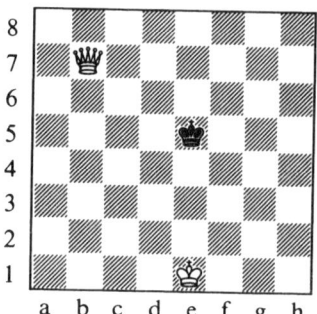

To his joy his opponent soon slipped up and lost his queen, and the following position was reached.

Ahmed was sure he was going to win. He had never checkmated with king and queen against king before but he would, no doubt, be able to work it out.

Being a bright boy he quickly got the idea of using his king and queen together to drive the enemy king to the corner of the board.

Then suddenly his opponent said, "Stalemate."

"What is stalemate?" asked Ahmed, "Is it the same as checkmate?"

64

This was the position.

Mr Jones, his teacher, who was watching the game, said, "No, it isn't. Stalemate is a draw."

Ahmed was very sad at only drawing his first game for the school but his teacher consoled him by saying that he had done very well.

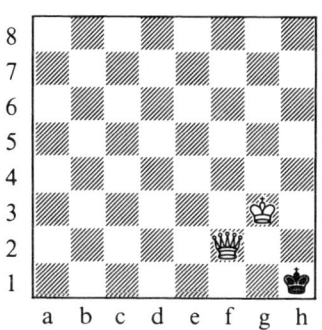

The following day Mr Jones called Ahmed over and said, "I'm now going to show you how to checkmate with king and queen against king, and I'll explain the difference between checkmate and stalemate." All the chess team gathered around and Mr Jones explained:

"This is an easy checkmate if you remember three rules.

1. Make sure that you don't **stalemate** the enemy king.

2. Your king and queen should work together as a team to drive the enemy king back.

3. Cut off the enemy king on any edge of the board.

Mr Jones then explained what stalemate was:

"If the king of the player whose turn it is to move is not in check and cannot move on to an adjacent square, because all the adjacent squares available to the king are attacked by enemy pieces, and if this player cannot move any other piece or pawn, then it is stalemate."

Now let us look at the three following positions.

65

Here, with White to move, the white king on h1 cannot move to any of the squares g1, g2 or h2 because these squares are attacked by enemy pieces and he would be moving into check. So White is stalemated and the game is drawn.

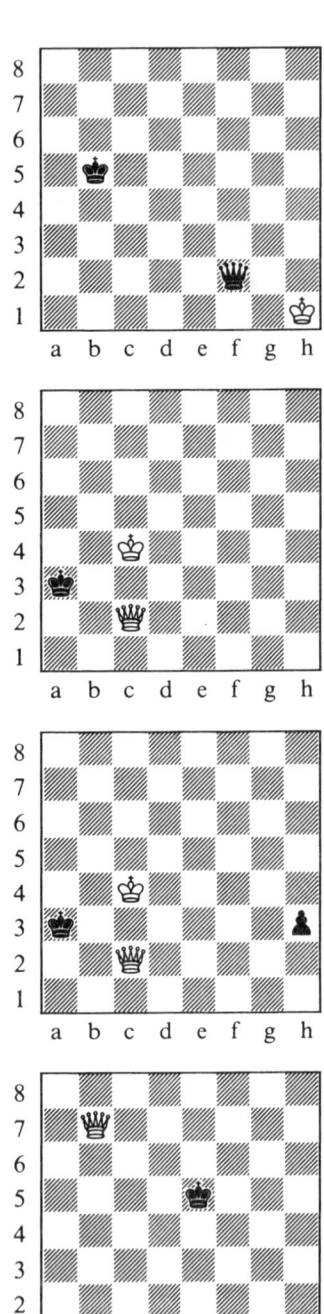

Here it is Black's turn but he cannot move without being in check, so he is stalemated and the game is drawn.

But here, with Black to move, the black king cannot move without being in check, but Black can move his pawn to h2, so this is not stalemate.

Now that you know about stalemate you should be very careful to see that you don't allow your opponent a stalemate position, because you will then only have drawn the game instead of winning it.

Now that we have learnt what stalemate is, we can learn the correct way to checkmate a king with a king and queen working together.

Look at this diagram and see what Ahmed should have played.

1.   Qc6

White brings his queen nearer to the centre to cut down the number of squares that Black can go to.

1.   ...   Kd4

Black tries to keep his king in the centre where it cannot be checkmated.

2.   Kd2

By placing his king opposite to the black king White leaves Black with only one square to move to.

We have now reached the position in the diagram.

2.   ...   Ke5

3.   Ke3

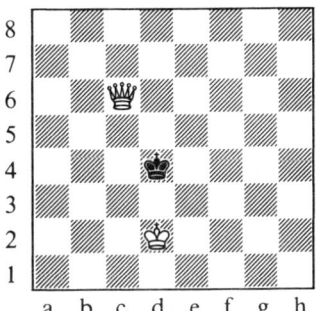

Forcing Black to move to the f-file and away from the centre of the board.

3.   ...   Kf5

Again the only move.

4.   Qd6

Notice how the king and queen are gradually forcing Black to move towards the h-file.

The diagram shows the position after 4. Qd6.

4.   ...   Kg4

The king must move to the g-file.

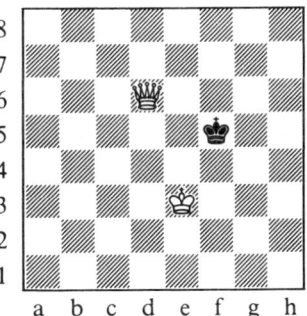

5.   Qg6 ch

Forcing the king onto the h-file – see the position in the diagram.

5.   ...   Kh4

Black has little choice.

6.   Kf3

The white king now moves in for the kill.

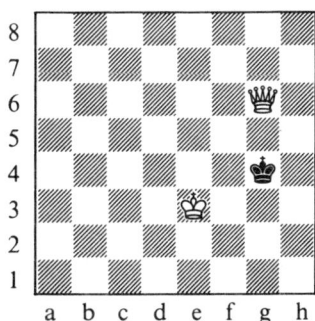

6.   ...   Kh3

Forced. We now have the position in this diagram.

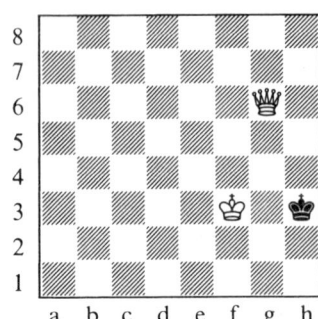

White has two ways of checkmating Black here. What are they?

a) **7. Qh7 mate.** Notice that the queen could have moved to any square on the h-file to give mate.

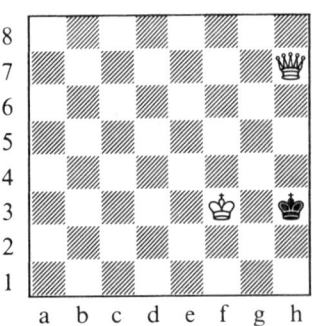

b) **7. Qg3 mate.**

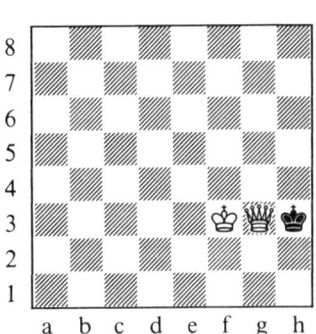

Exercise 12

(see answers in Chapter 22)

1. Which of the two positions below is stalemate?

2. Why is the other position not stalemate?

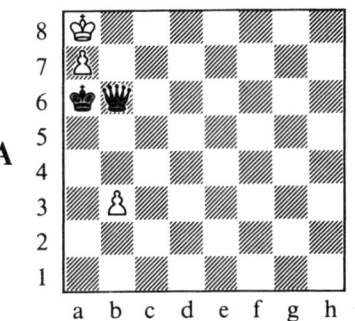

3. White to move and mate. It should not take you more than five moves.

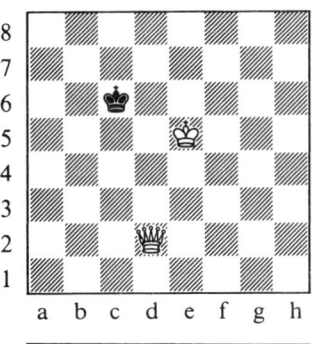

4. Black to move and draw in one move. Look out for stalemating chances.

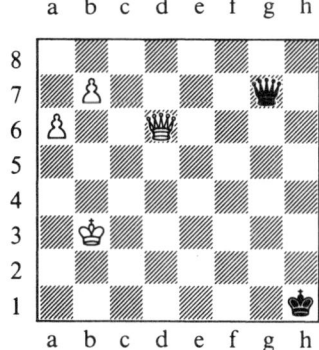

Chapter 13

KING AND ROOK AGAINST KING

Ahmed and the other members of the team listened attentively to Mr Jones's explanation of how to mate with king and queen against king and quickly grasped the way to go about it.

At the next session of the school chess club John Lisowski, the best player in the school, asked Mr Jones, "Is it possible to checkmate with king and any piece?" Mr Jones replied, "You can checkmate with king and rook but you can't checkmate with king and bishop or king and knight. I'll now show you how to checkmate with king and rook."

Mr Jones went on to explain that first you must know the mating position. The enemy king is always driven to the edge of the board and the rook gives checkmate when the two kings are facing each other (as in the diagram).

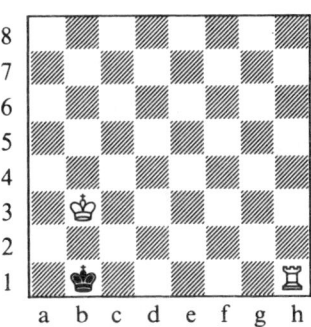

To reach this position the king and rook must work together to force the king back.

You must first decide which rank or file the enemy king is to be checkmated on.

In this position White decides to checkmate along the rank a1-h1.

White to move plays

1.   Rg3

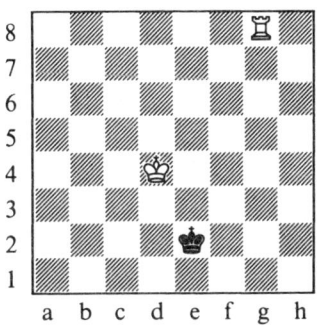

This cuts off the black king, which can now only play on the first two ranks, a1-h1 and a2-h2.

1. ... **Kf2**

Attacking the rook.

2. Ra3

Moving it as far away as possible from the black king.

2. ... **Ke2**

Staying near the centre of the board, where he cannot be checkmated.

3. Rb3

An important waiting move to force the black king to move opposite to the white king.

If instead White played 3. Ke4 then after 3. ... Kd2 4. Kd4 Ke2 he would have made no progress.

This is the position after White's waiting move 3. Rb3.

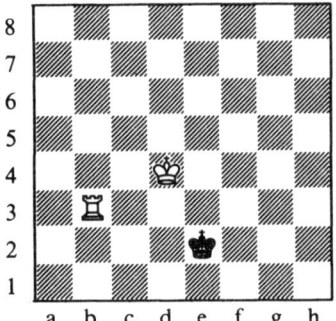

3.	...	**Kf2**
4.	**Ke4**	**Kg2**
5.	**Kf4**	**Kh2**
6.	**Kg4**	**Kg2**

The black king has been forced to move opposite to White's king.

7. Rb2 ch

When the two kings are opposite to each other, the rook must check.

This is the position after 7 Rb2 ch.

Black must move to the first rank and White can repeat his plan.

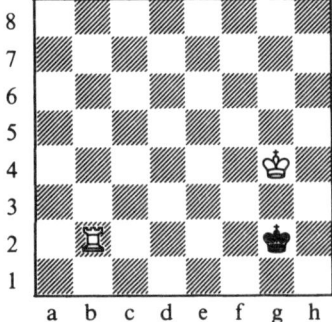

7.	...	**Kf1**
8.	**Kf3**	**Ke1**
9.	**Rh2**	

Another waiting move to force Black to place his king opposite to White's.

This is the position after 9. Rh2.

If Black now plays 9. ... Kf1 then White replies 10. Rh1 mate.

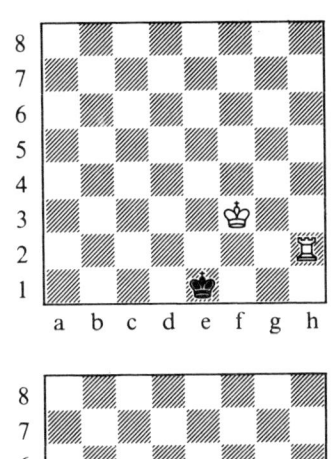

9.	...	Kd1
10.	Ke3	Kc1
11.	Kd3	Kb1
12.	Kc3	Ka1
13.	Kb3	Kb1
14.	Rh1 mate	

This is the final position after 14. Rh1 mate.

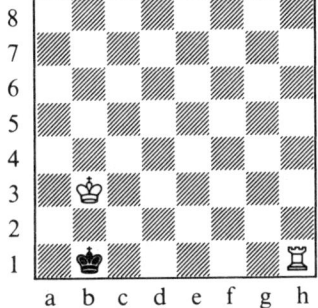

THREE IMPORTANT THINGS TO REMEMBER

1 Your king and rook must work together.

2 To force Black's king opposite to White's you must play a waiting move.

3 When the two kings are opposite to each other you must check with your rook.

This way of checkmating with king and rook is not the quickest but is the easiest to learn.

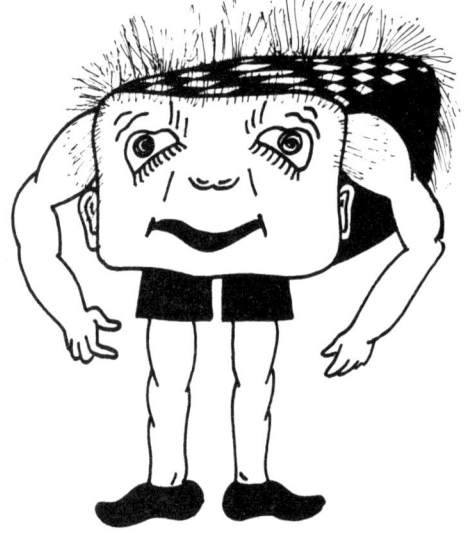

That was a very difficult checkmate, but learning it will make you a winner.

Exercise 13

(see answers in Chapter 22)

White to move and mate in the two positions below.

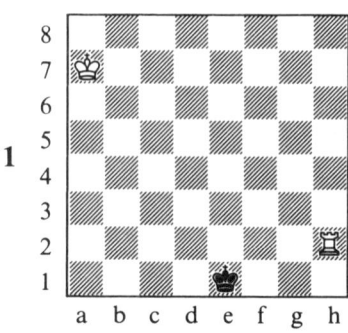

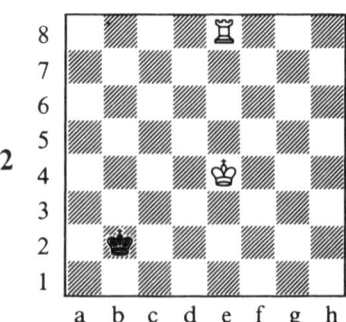

Chapter 14

DOUBLE ATTACKS, FORKS AND PINS

Taking enemy pieces often helps you to win the game. If you can attack two enemy pieces at the same time like the dragon on page 76 you will usually be able to capture one of them on your next move. This tactic is called **double attack**. Here are some examples.

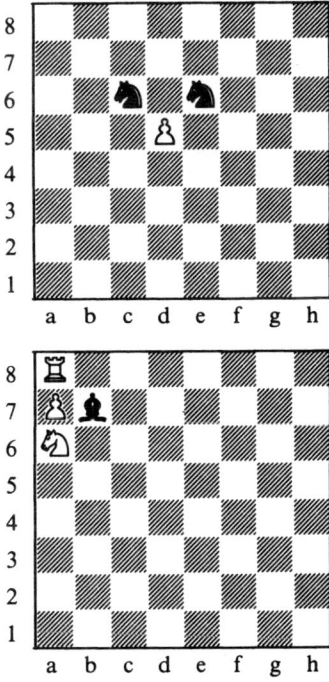

The white pawn on d5 is attacking both black knights. Only one of them can move away, so the other will be captured on White's next move.

The bishop will capture either the rook or knight on Black's next move.

A very dangerous double attack is seen here. Since the king must move the queen is lost.

A double attack by the knight is called a 'fork'.

As the queen can travel on ranks, files and diagonals it can double attack well.

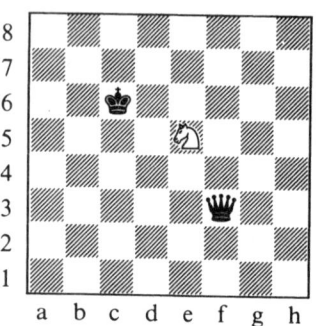

Here the double attack on the king and knight will win the knight.

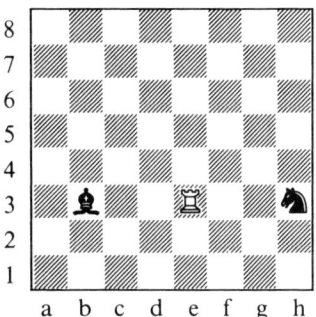

The rook attacks the bishop and knight along the third rank.

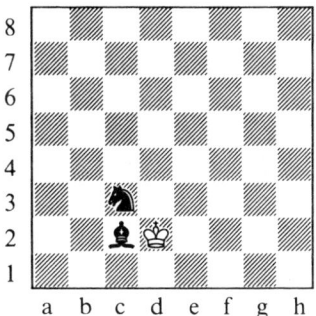

The king can also be used to double attack, but great care must be taken to avoid the danger of checkmate.

Here the double attack by the king wins one of the pieces.

THE HELPLESS MESSENGER

Keith, the faithful messenger of the queen, spurred his horse on to full gallop in an effort to reach King Edward and warn him of the treacherous ambush on the road ahead. But alas, his efforts were going to be in vain, for his way was suddenly blocked by three horsemen, armed to the teeth, who quickly surrounded him, forced him to dismount and pulled him behind a bush where he was pinned against a rock with a spear against his ribs. He was helpless to save the king and could do nothing but watch sadly as his monarch walked into the trap.

PINS

Just as Keith could not move when he was pinned, so a chess piece which is pinned cannot move and cannot take an enemy piece.

The knight on d4 in the diagram cannot move away because the king would be in check to the bishop, and this is against the rules. The bishop is pinning the knight.

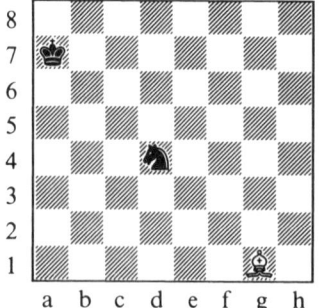

Here the rook is pinning the bishop against the king so that the bishop cannot move to capture the queen on its diagonal.

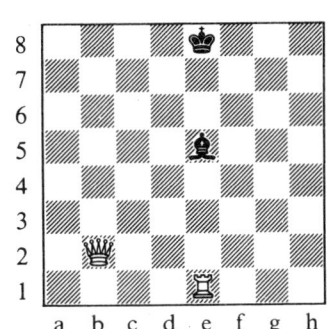

White is able to play the surprise move Qh6 ch because the pawn on g7 is pinned by the bishop on b2. The queen on h6 cannot be taken and it is checkmate on the next move.

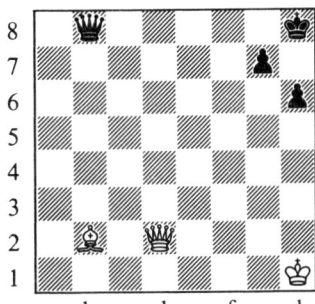

Here White plays Qe8 checkmate! The black knight on f6 cannot take the queen because it is pinned by the bishop on g5.

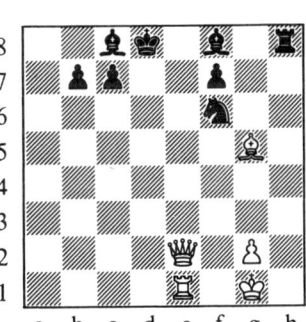

In this diagram there is an interesting example of a pin by a rook on the d-file. White to move plays Qg7 and Black cannot take the white queen as his rook is pinned to the king by the white rook on d1.

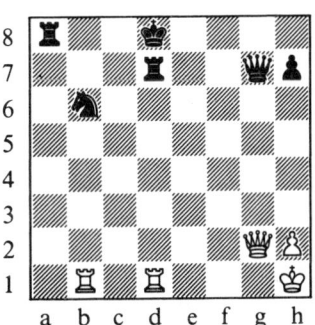

Exercise 14

(see answers in Chapter 22)

1. White has just played Ne5, winning a pawn. It is Black to move. Is there a double attack?

2. Black to play. Can you find a fork?

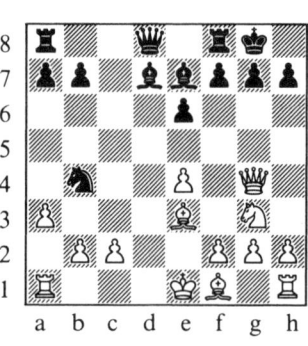

3. White to move and win a piece by a double attack.

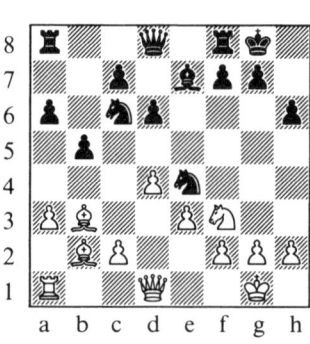

4. White to move. Can you use a pin to win a piece?

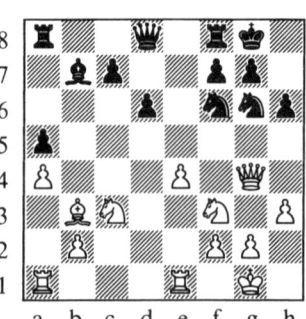

Chapter 15

THE SKEWER, DISCOVERED CHECK AND DOUBLE DISCOVERED CHECK

SITTING BULL WINS AGAIN

Sitting Bull, the cunning Sioux chief, waited behind the rock for his Apache enemy to come within range.

Two young braves were walking quietly along the trail. One was right behind the other. They were unaware of any danger.

Sitting Bull weighed up the situation in a flash and made his plan. He would wait until they were almost upon him, then fire his arrow at point blank range so that there would be no time for both of them

to get out of the way. If he missed the one in front he would hit the one behind.

It worked perfectly. His aim was true and fast, but the first brave just had time to get out of the way. The second brave dropped to the ground groaning and clutching at the arrow in his side.

We have just seen that the chief was successful because he attacked two men on the same path. In chess an attack on two pieces on the same line is called a skewer. The piece nearest to the attacker is forced to move, leaving the way clear for the attacker to take the other piece.

Here are some examples.

The black rook has checked the white king, which is forced to move. The black rook can then take the white knight.

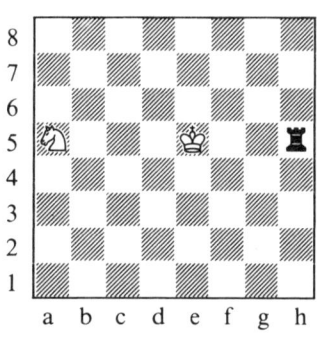

Here the black bishop checks the white king and then wins the white queen behind it.

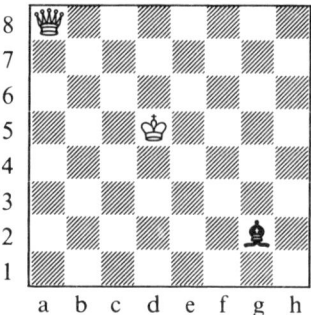

The black queen is attacked by the white bishop allowing the win of the black rook. Of course the queen could either capture the bishop or stay where she is, but then the very important queen would have been lost for the much less valuable bishop.

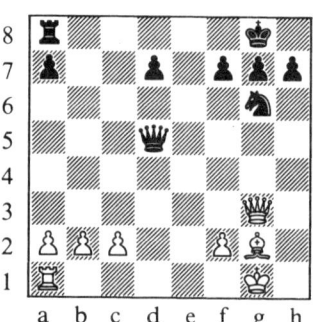

82

THE SET-UP

Jake the crook was pleased. The old watchman had believed his story and was unsuspectingly leading him to the strongroom where the diamonds were kept. "If I can pull off this snatch I'll be rich for life," he thought. Good, the old man had opened up the combination lock. All that remained was to enter the room, cosh the old man, scoop up the famous Vanderbilt diamonds and stroll nonchalantly downstairs to the getaway car.

So he followed the old man into the room; but suddenly there was an unexpected development. The old man threw himself to one side and Jake found himself facing an imposing looking man who was pointing a revolver at him.

"Good evening, Jake. I've been expecting you. My name is Inspector Booth, and you're under arrest."

83

DISCOVERED CHECK

Just as Jake was surprised by the watchman and Inspector Booth, so there are many chess players caught out by discovered check.

Discovered check is when one piece on the same line as the enemy king moves out of the way to allow another piece behind to check the enemy king. It is another form of double attack, and here are some examples.

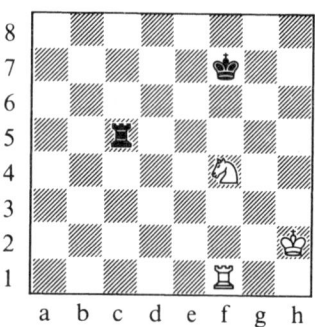

When the white knight moves to d3 the rook on f1 is checking the black king on f7. If Black moves his king to avoid check then the knight will capture the rook on c5 next move. If Black plays Rf5 then White plays Rf5 ch winning the black rook. Discovered checks often surprise an opponent and win material.

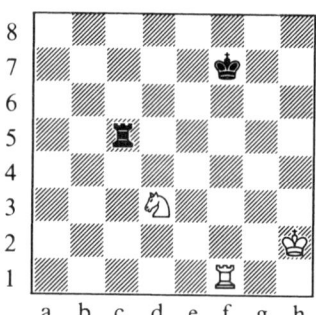

This is the position when the knight has moved to d3.

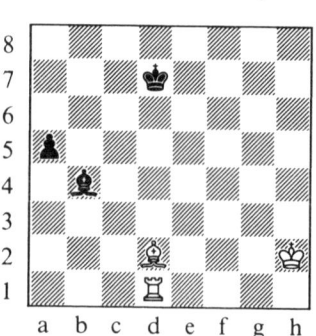

Here it looks as though Black's bishop is guarded by his pawn on a5.

But when White plays Bb4 the black king is in check and the pawn cannot take the bishop because Black must move his king.

84

This is the position after the bishop capture.

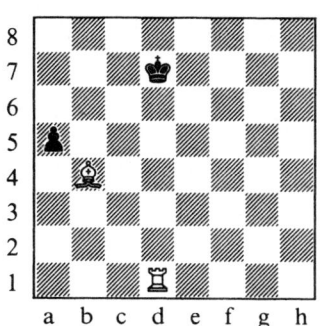

DOUBLE DISCOVERED CHECK

The two strangers were showing the king the way across the marshes. They led the way in single file with the king behind. Suddenly one moved to one side and pointed his dagger at the king, and at the same time the other man drew his sword and advanced menacingly towards the king. The king was completely taken by surprise and suddenly his life was in real danger, because he knew that it was going to be difficult to defend himself successfully against the threats of both of them.

Double discovered check in chess is like this too. It happens when a piece that moves allows an attack from another piece behind it and at the same time attacks the enemy king itself. This can be very unpleasant for the king that is attacked. Here are two examples.

85

Black plays Be4 and both the rook and the bishop are checking the king at the same time.

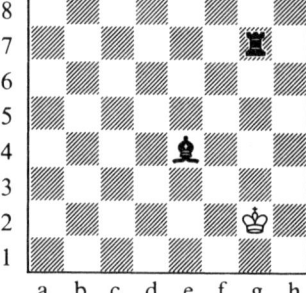

The position after Be4 ch looks like this.

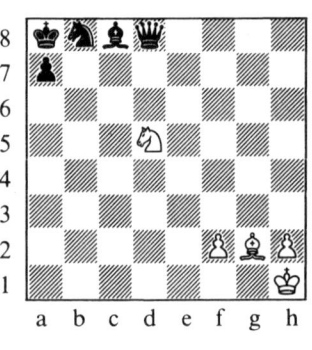

Double discovered check can sometimes lead to checkmate as the king is forced to move and two pieces are attacking the squares around it.

In this diagram White can play Nc7 or Nb6 double ch and mate.

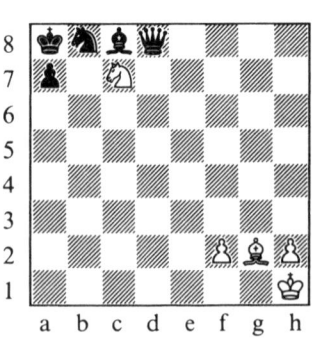

Here is the position after Nc7 with the king checkmated.

Exercise 15

(see answers in Chapter 22)

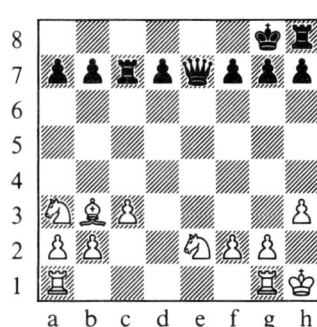

1. Can Black safely capture White's knight on e2?

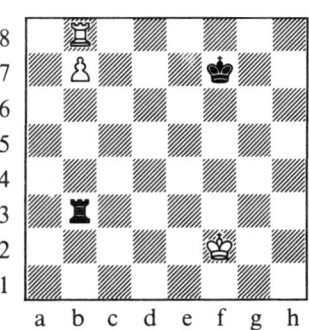

2. White to move and win. Here is a clue – if White moves his rook can Black safely take the white pawn? Look out for skewer chances.

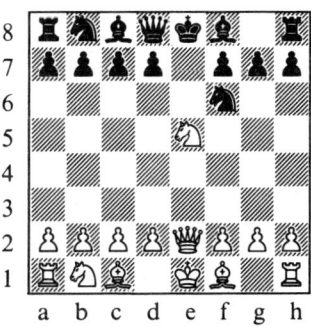

3. Can White win Black's queen?

4. What is White's best move?

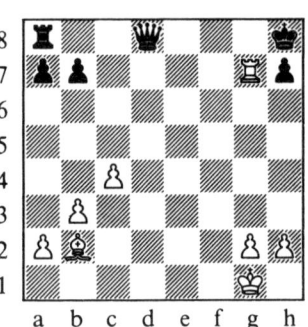

5. White to move and mate.

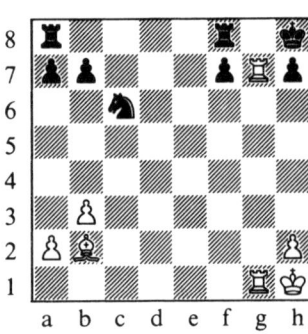

6. White to move and mate.

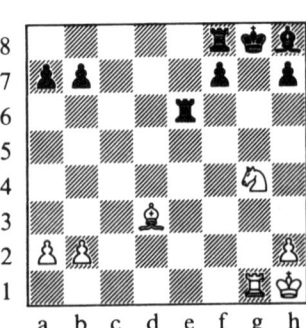

88

Chapter 16

COMBINATIONS AND SACRIFICES

John Andrews was pleased. He couldn't believe his luck – he'd been drawn to play against a girl in the semi-final of the Parkhill District Junior Chess Championship. He didn't know her but it was bound to be easy. "Girls can't play chess," he thought.

So half an hour later he strolled confidently to the board to meet his opponent, Helen Smith, a rather quiet and timid mouse of a girl.

John introduced himself and said, "I'm John, hope we have a good game." The girl replied, "Me too, I'm Helen," and play began.

John, who had the black pieces, played a defence called the Sicilian which his teacher had taught him only the other day. He thought, "That'll fox her, she'll never have seen this defence before!"

After a few moves the position in the diagram was reached.

John was already confident and pleased with his position. She'd given him a pawn for nothing on the last move – she couldn't be very good.

Suddenly Helen played Bf7 ch and John smiled. Just what he'd expected, giving away her pieces for nothing. He quickly removed Helen's bishop. Then he took another look at the board and froze. Now he saw why she'd played Bf7 ch. It was a sacrifice which won his queen. Helen took the queen on d8 with her own queen and quickly mopped up the rest of John's pieces.

Never again would John underestimate girls. He had even more respect for Helen when she went on to win the championship.

In her game with John Helen played a **combination** when she sacrificed her bishop to win John's queen.

Quite simply, a combination is when one player chooses a line of play which leads to the exchange or sacrifice of some of his pieces or pawns in order to gain an advantage.

This diagram shows a simple example. White plays 1. Rf6, giving up a rook worth 5 points for a knight worth only 3 points. Why? Because he has seen that after 1. Rf6 gf6 he can play 2. Qh7 mate.

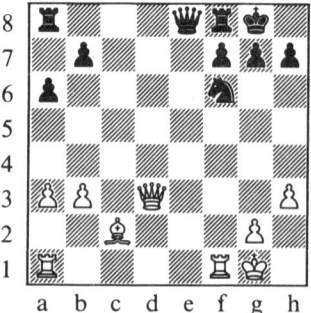

OVERLOAD COMBINATIONS

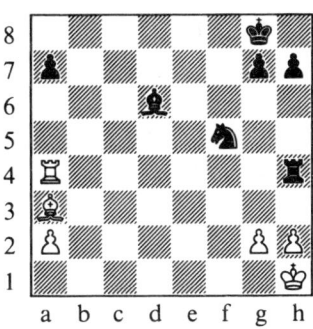

This position shows an 'overload' combination. What does this mean?

The black knight is guarding both the rook on h4 and the bishop on d6. It has too much to do – it is overloaded with work. So White plays 1. Rh4 Nh4 2. Bd6 and he wins a piece.

A piece can be overloaded when it has the task of guarding **at the same time** one of its own pieces **and** a vital square.

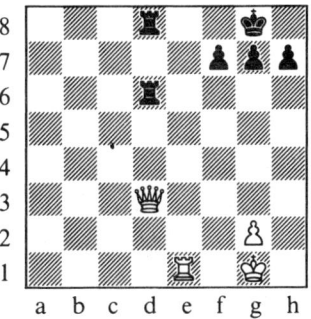

Here the black rook on d8 is guarding the rook on d6 and at the same time stopping the white rook from mating on e8. So White can play 1. Qd6 Rd6 2. Re8 mate.

The black rook had one job too many.

This position is more difficult.

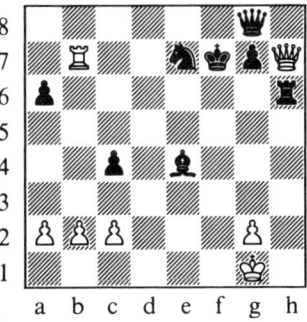

At first sight it looks as if Black is winning easily. He has an extra bishop and knight, and his king looks safe surrounded by his own pieces. He thinks, "If White plays 1. Qg8 ch then I can play 1. ... Kg8 and after 2. Re7 Bc2 I will still be winning." But his king is overloaded and White plays instead 1. Re7 ch Ke7 2. Qg8, and now White is winning. If 1. Re7 ch Kf8 then 2. Re8 ch Ke8 3. Qg8 ch wins easily for White.

So overload combinations can be found in unexpected positions. Look out for them!

DECOY SACRIFICES

In this position Black looks to be on top but White produces an unpleasant surprise.

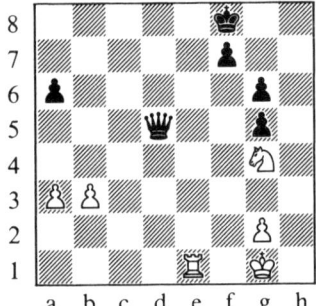

1. Re8 ch	Ke8	or	1. Re8 ch	Kg7
2. Nf6 ch	Kd7		2. Rg8 ch	Kg8

3. Nd5 capturing the 3. Nf6 ch winning
queen and winning   the queen

This position looks about level, with both sides having the same number of pieces and pawns. But Black sees a chance to deliver a knockout punch with:

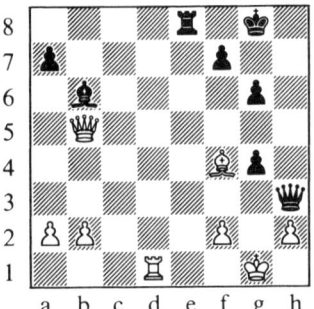

1. ...	Bf2 ch or	1. ...	Bf2 ch
2. Kf2	Qf3 ch	2. Kf2	Qf3 ch
3. Kg1	Qd1 ch	3. Kg1	Qd1 ch
4. Qf1	Re1	4. Kf2	Qf3 ch
winning the queen		5. Kg1	Re1 ch
		6. Qf1	Rf1 mate

This position shows another decoy combination with a surprise in store for Black.

Black is already counting this position as won, thinking that after 1. ef8=Q ch Kf8 his rook and extra pawn will win the game.

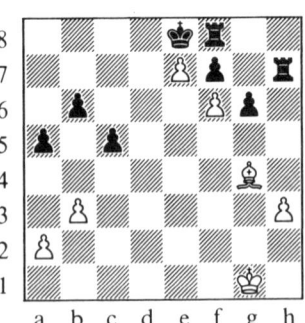

92

But White plays the surprise sacrifice
1. Bd7 ch Kd7 2. ef8=N ch Kd6 3. Nh7
and wins.

So the decoy sacrifice of the bishop
won both rooks and the game.

In this position White has a strong
attack but it is hard to see how he can win.
He plays the unexpected 1. Be6, which
looks a bad blunder as his queen on h6
can now be captured by the black queen.
But really it is an excellent move which
threatens to win the queen and the game
by Rg8 ch after

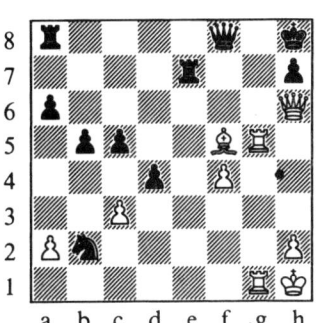

1. Be6	Qh6	or	1. Be6	Re6
2. Rg8 ch	Rg8		2. Qe6	Re8
3. Rg8 mate			3. Rg8 ch	Qg8
			4. Qf6 ch	Qg7
			5. Qg7 mate	

PROMOTION SACRIFICES

When a pawn is well forward, on the
fifth, sixth or seventh ranks, it is
sometimes possible to sacrifice one of
your pieces to help it become a queen.

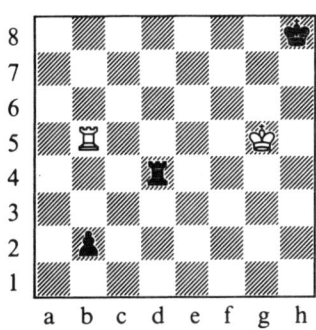

Here Black's pawn is just one square
away from queening but it is threatened
by White's rook on b5. Black's best move
seems to be Rd2, but there is another
possibility. 1. ... Rd5 ch 2. Rd5 (otherwise
he will lose the rook) 2. ... b1=Q and the
pawn queens and Black is winning.

93

This position looks fairly level as White has a knight and two pawns against a rook. But Black has a promotion combination. 1. ... Rg2 ch 2. Ng2 h3, and the knight cannot stop the pawn from queening.

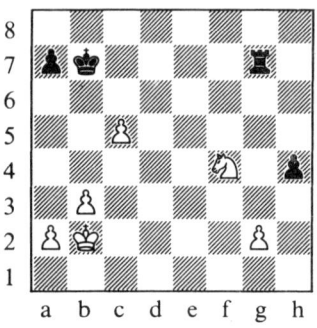

If the knight doesn't capture the rook then the rook will help the pawn to become a queen or force the knight to take the pawn in a position where the rook can then recapture the knight.

From now on, in your games you should look out for a chance to play the different kinds of combination we have met. If you do, you will be a far more dangerous opponent to play against.

Exercise 16

(see answers in Chapter 22)

1. White to move and win a piece. Look out for a sacrifice and a skewer.

2. Black to move and mate in two moves.

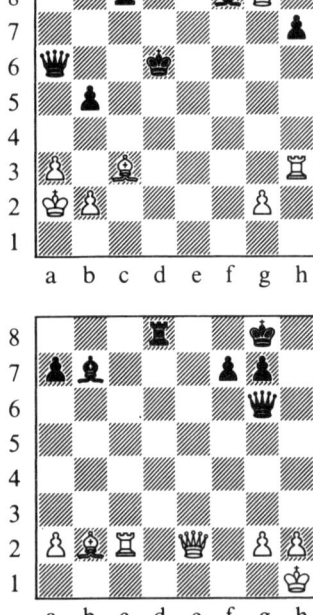

3. White to move and mate in two moves.

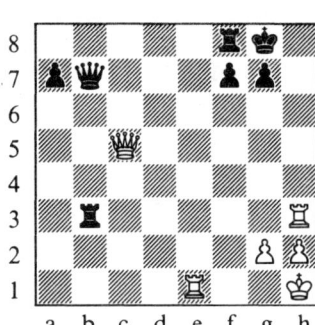

4. White to mate in five moves. Look out for a bishop sacrifice.

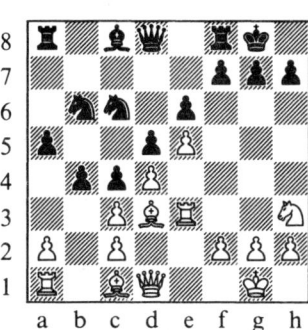

5. Black to move and win a piece in three moves. Look out for a queen sacrifice and a knight fork.

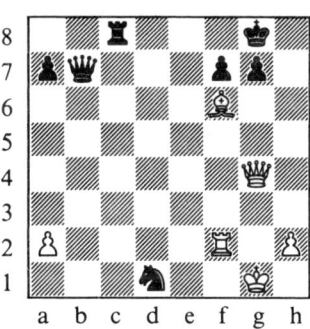

6. White to mate in two moves. Is there a sacrifice which would help?

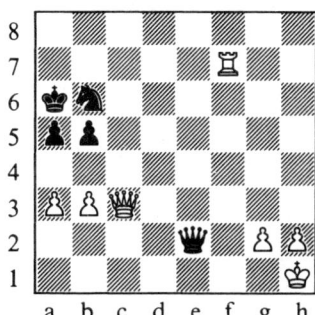

Chapter 17

ATTACKING THE CASTLED KING

Always treat your opponent with respect

Roger Carstairs, the sixteen year old champion of the famous Dunford School team, was really annoyed. He had been looking forward with pleasant anticipation to the tough match with the Marton's School number one, John Delaney. Unfortunately John had been taken ill and they had substituted an eleven year old kid called Wesley Garner. How dare they! Fancy wasting his time.

Roger showed his contempt by not speaking to Wesley and by moving as soon as his opponent made a move.

Just as expected he quickly won rook for bishop, and he sat back with a superior air looking disdainfully at the youngster. This was the position with Wesley to move.

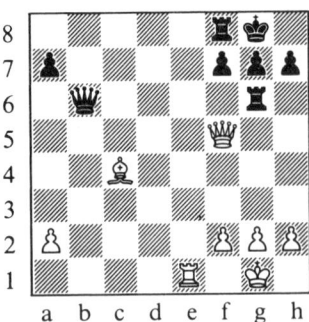

Roger thought, "What's he wasting time on? Why is he taking so long?" Then, "I know, he doesn't want to be beaten long before the rest of his team. Poor kid, they certainly overmatched him this time." He took another look at the position and thought, "He has no attack and my king is absolutely safe tucked behind those pawns. I've only to get my other rook into the game and it will all be over in no time."

Wesley then picked up his queen and held it in the air for about a minute before playing

Qf7 ch

Roger's first thought was, "I didn't know he was that bad – fancy blundering away his queen." Then he took another look and his face went white. He couldn't believe it. He was lost, because if he played Kh8 then Qf8 was mate, and if he played Rf7 then Re8 was mate!

Wesley held out his hand and said, "Thanks for the game. These back row mates certainly need watching."

In a daze Roger shook hands and slunk from the room without looking at anyone and went straight home to recover.

From Wesley's win we can learn that three unmoved pawns in front of a castled king can be a weakness because the king cannot escape from the back rank if he is checked.

Another example of this back row weakness is shown in this diagram.

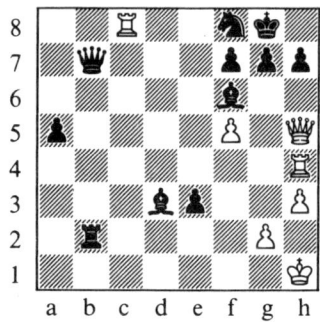

Black looks to be a certain winner. He is threatening mate in one with Qg2, both White's rooks are attacked, Black has two extra pieces and his pawn on e3 seems likely to become a queen in two moves. His own king's position looks safe as houses.

White's only threat is the attack by queen and rook on the h-pawn, and that seems to be well protected by the knight on f8. But incredibly White to move can mate on h7 with his queen because the knight on f8 cannot recapture; it is pinned to its king by the enemy rook on c8. Placing the queen in front of one of her own rooks or bishops is a good way of attacking the three pawns in front of the enemy king.

Here it looks as though Black can just survive the trouble on the diagonal a1-h8. 1. Rg7 ch Kh8 and if now 2. Rg2 ch (a discovered check by the bishop on b2) guarding the bishop, Black can play 2. ... f6 cutting out the check. If instead 1. Rg7 ch Kh8 2. Rf7 ch then 2. ... Qb2 3. Rf8 ch Kg7 and Black will win with his pawn on c4.

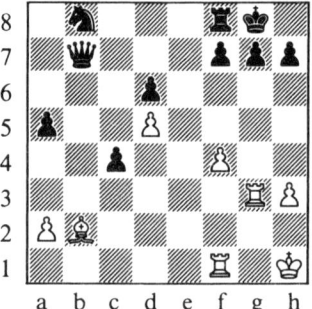

But White comes up with the unexpected 1. Rg7 ch Kh8 2. Rg8 double discovered check Kg8 (forced, as both the rook and the bishop are checking the king) 3. Rg1 mate.

So look out for piece sacrifices as a way of breaking down the three pawns defence in front of the castled king.

KNIGHT'S PAWN ONE SQUARE FORWARD

This position of the pawns can leave a weakness on the black squares when Black has castled on the kingside.

In position **A** White's queen and pawn take advantage of the holes on the white squares to mate at b7.

In position **B** White's queen and bishop prove a deadly combination on the diagonal a1-h8.

In position **C** the bishop and knight alone mate because of the weaknesses at a3 and c3.

In position **D** the knight checks and mates on e2 with the help of the queen.

Notice that in all four positions gaping holes for the attacking pieces to enter have been left by playing the knight's pawn forward.

If Black's bishop had been placed on g7 in 'B' the queen could not have entered. So it is a good idea to keep a bishop between these pawns to prevent pieces from moving into the holes.

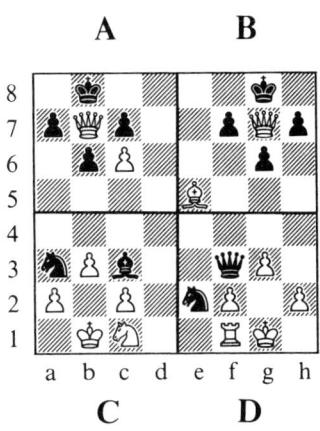

Here White is about to play his bishop to h6. He wants to swap it for the black bishop on g7. When he has done this Black's king position will be less secure and easier to attack later on.

Another way of attacking when the knight's pawn has been moved is to move forward your own rook's pawn to h4 then h5 and swap off the rook's pawn for the knight's pawn.

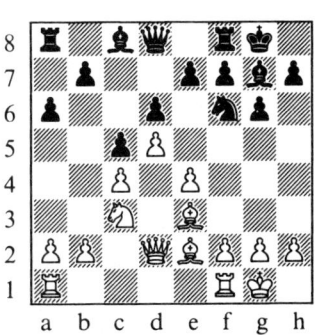

Here Black is a pawn up but with White to move he cannot prevent mate by the white queen on h7 after hg6.

White's chances were greatly improved in the above example because he had four pieces attacking and Black had only one solitary bishop defending. The same thing happens in football – if there are four forwards and only one defender a goal is likely. So when you attack, do so with as many pieces as possible.

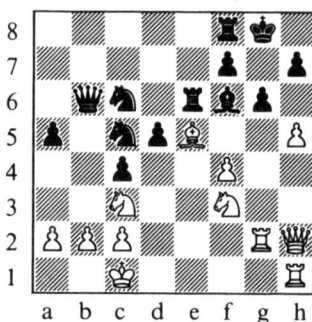

ROOK'S PAWN ONE SQUARE FORWARD

When the rook's pawn has moved one square forward it becomes a target for attack.

Here it is White to move.

He can safely capture the h6 pawn with his bishop, because after 1. Bh6 gh6 2. Qh6 ch Kg8 3. Rg1 ch Qg7 4. Qg7 is mate.

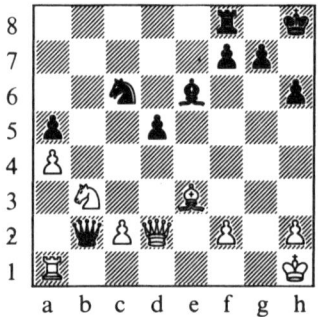

The rook's pawn can also be attacked by the knight's pawn.

Here White plays 1. g5. If Black doesn't capture the g-pawn he will lose at least a pawn; and after 1. .... hg5 2. Rg5 White has opened up both the g-file and the h-file.

From these two positions we learn to look out for chances of attacking the castled king position with the h-pawn one square forward by either sacrificing a piece or exchanging a pawn to open up the g-file and h-file.

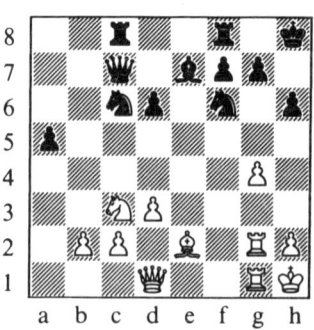

Once the h-file has been opened up the chances of checkmating are good. Look at this diagram for four examples of checkmate which happen because the h-pawn is missing. It is White to move and to mate in one each time.

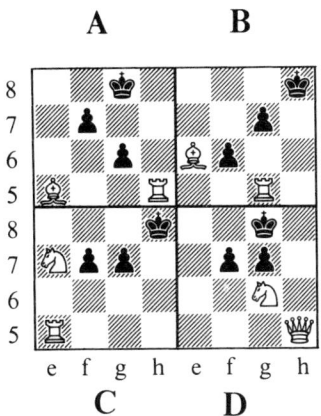

A Rh8 mate

B Rh5 mate

C Rh5 mate

D Qh8 mate

From these positions we learn that a missing rook's pawn is a very serious matter and gives good winning chances to the other side. So be on the look-out for a chance to get rid of your opponent's rook's pawn.

ISOLATED PAWNS AROUND THE KING

The last pawn position we will look at is when the pawns have been separated from each other.

In this diagram White's pawns stand side by side; they are what we call **united** pawns.

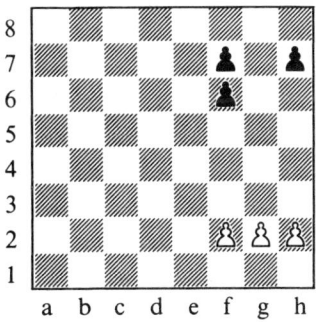

If one of them is attacked it can move forward and it will be supported by its brothers. For example, if the f-pawn is attacked on f2 it can move forward to f3 where it will be defended by the pawn on g2. So united pawns are good because they can support each other.

Now look at Black's pawns. The two pawns on f6 and f7 are **doubled** pawns. They are called doubled pawns because they both stand on the same file. They also stand apart from the h-pawn.

When pawns stand alone with no pawn on the file to either side they are called **isolated** pawns. All three black pawns in this diagram are isolated pawns. They suffer from the weakness that they cannot defend each other.

Isolated and doubled pawns in front of the castled king are especially bad and make it much harder for the player who has them to defend his king.

Take a look at the four positions in this diagram. In each case White can give mate in one move.

A   Qh7 mate

B   Qg7 mate

C   Bf6 mate

D   Nf6 mate

In all four positions the white pieces were able to get very near to the black king because the pawns were isolated and/or doubled.

So look out for ways of giving your opponent doubled and isolated pawns. It will give you excellent attacking chances.

Exercise 17

(see answers in Chapter 22)

1.   White to move and win in two moves.

2.   Black to move and win in two moves.

3.   White to move and mate in two moves.

4.   White to move and mate in three moves. Look out for a queen sacrifice.

5.   White to move and win in three moves. How can you get at Black's

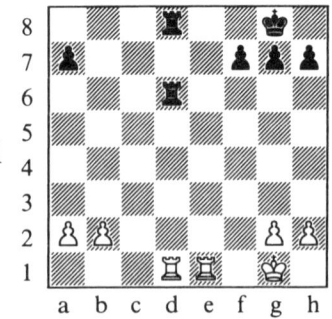

102

king with a sacrifice?

6. White to move and win in three moves.

7. White to move and win in three moves. Can you get at Black's king with a sacrifice?

8. Black to move and win in four moves. How best can you use the two black rooks on the seventh rank?

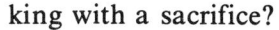

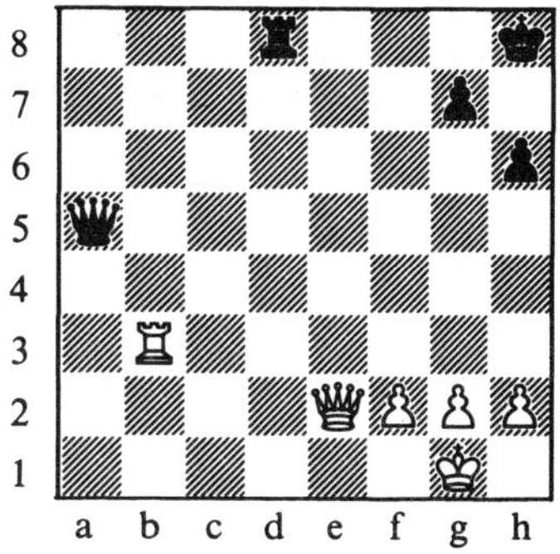

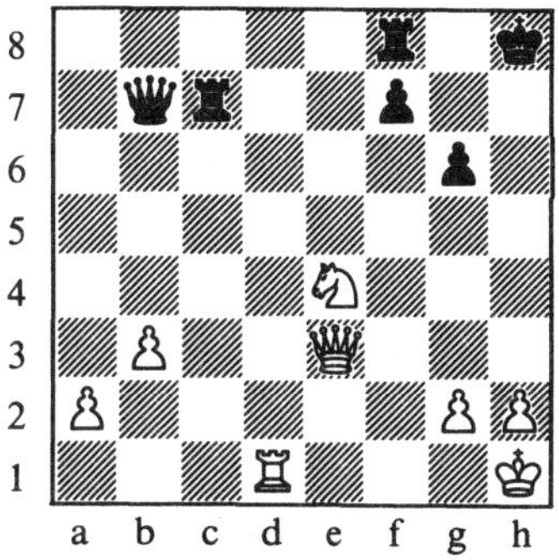

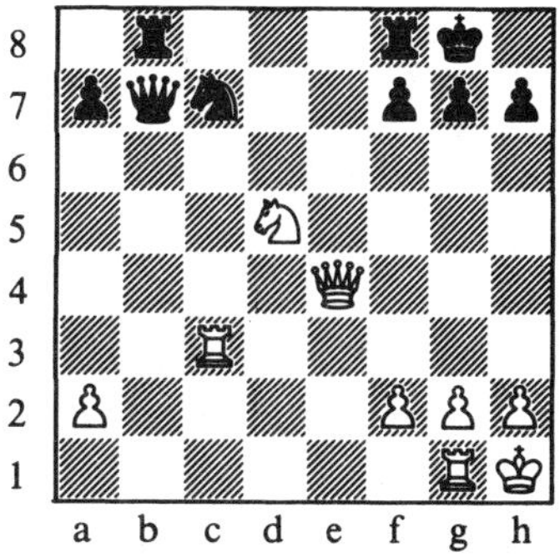

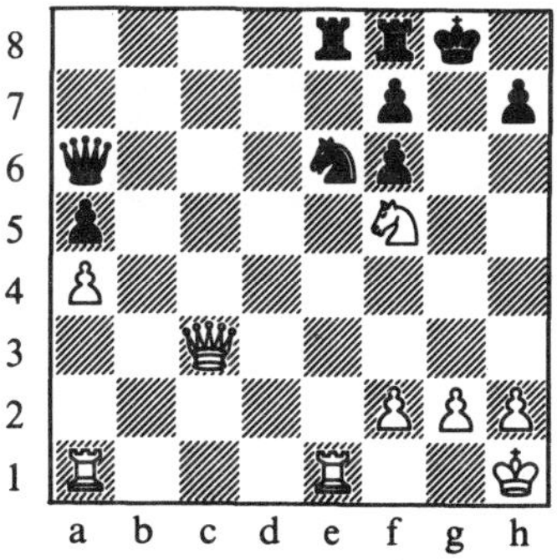

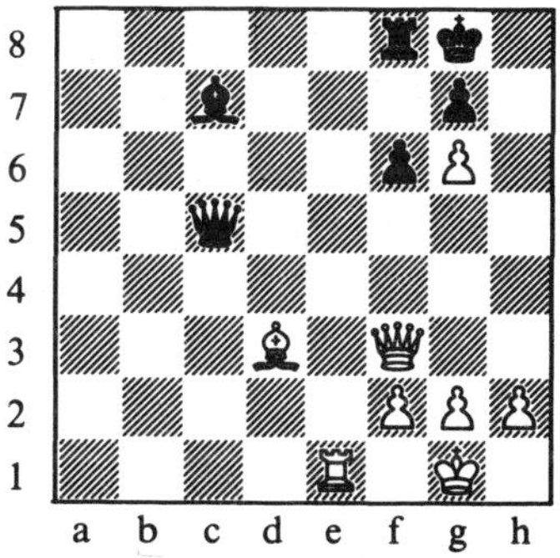

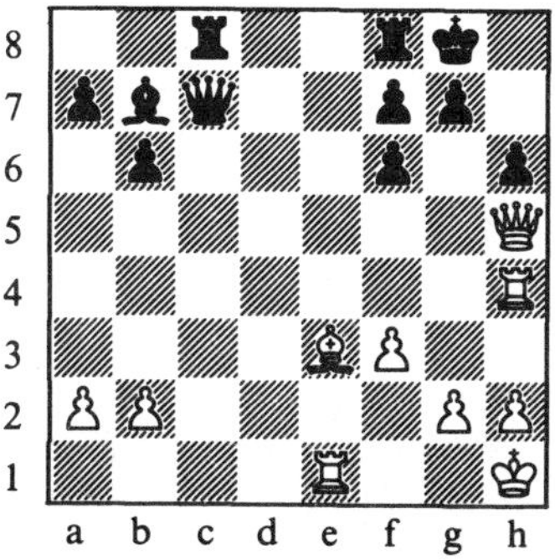

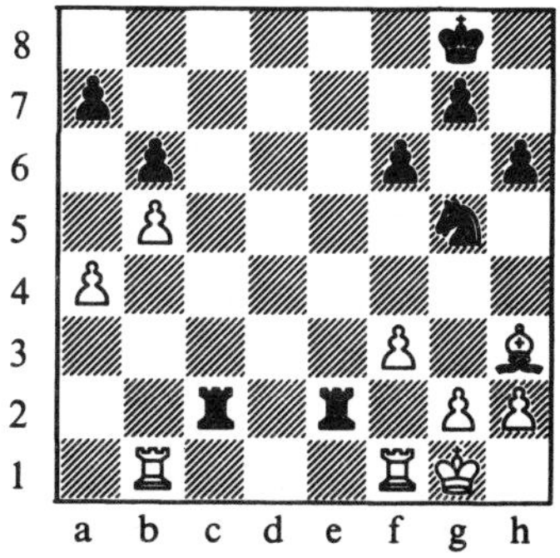

Chapter 18

HOW TO PLAY THE OPENINGS

Here are a few useful tips.

a) Try to put **either** your king's pawn or your queen's pawn or **both** pawns on the squares e4 and d4 respectively.

b) Try to place your pieces on squares in the centre of the board where they can attack the enemy army.

c) Castle early in the game in order to get your king out of the way of enemy attacks and place your rooks in the centre where they can attack.

d) Always play moves which have a purpose and which you understand.

e) Play the King's Pawn openings until you have been playing for some time. They are easier to understand.

We will now look at an opening called the Centre Game to see how these tips work out in practice.

WHITE	*BLACK*

1.   e4

This is a good opening move because it allows White to bring out his king's bishop and queen. Also the pawn on e4 controls the important squares d5 and f5.

1.   ...   e5

Black decides that it is a good idea to move his king's pawn too.

2.   d4

This move attacks Black's e-pawn and allows White's queen's bishop to come into play. It also gives the queen another two squares to move to, d2 and d3.

2.   ...   ed4

Why does Black capture? He has seen that after Qd4 he can play Nc6, so . . .

3.   Qd4   Nc6

This is an excellent move as it not only develops a piece in the centre of the board but also attacks the white queen, forcing it to move again and so gaining time.

4.   Qe3

White keeps his queen well placed in the centre and also guards the e-pawn.

4.   ...   Nf6

Developing his knight on a good square near to the centre and preparing to attack the e-pawn.

5.   Nc3

Developing and defending the e-pawn.

5.   ...   Bb4

105

Developing his bishop and pinning the white knight to the white king.

In the position in the diagram Black has three pieces in play and White only two pieces. So White must be very careful.

6.   Bd2

Wisely breaking the pin by developing his bishop.

6.   ...   O-O

Black takes his king to safety and brings his rook into play.

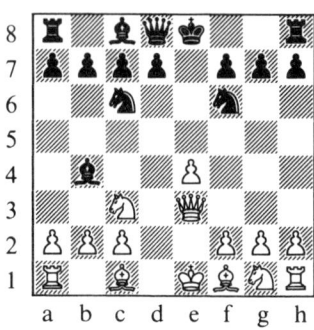

If White now plays 7. e5 Black will play 7. ... Ne5 8. Qe5 Re8 pinning the queen and winning queen for rook.

If White doesn't see the threat on his e-pawn and plays 7. Nf3, Black can play 7. ... Bc3 8. Bc3 Ne4 9. Qe4 Re8 10. Ne5 Ne5 11. Be5 d6 winning back the piece and remaining a pawn ahead.

7.   O-O-O

White sees the threats on his king's pawn and gets out of the way fast. His own queen's rook is now well placed to join in the game with play on the d-file.

7.   ...   Re8

Black's rook is now attacking the e-pawn.

8.   Bc4

This is a very interesting move. White is prepared to give up his e-pawn for a dangerous attack.

In the position in the diagram Black can try to win the king's pawn in two ways:

a) 8. ... Bc3 9. Bc3 Re4 10. Bf6 Re3
    11. Bd8 Re8 12. Bc7 and White has
    won a piece and a pawn.

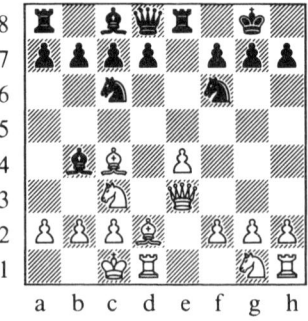

106

b) 8. ... Bc3 9. Bc3 Ne4 10. Qf4 (this threatens Bf7 ch followed by Be8) 10. ... Nf6 11. Nf3 d6 12. Ng5 and White has a fierce attack for the pawn.

Back in 1896 World Champion Wilhelm Steinitz lost with the black pieces from this position, so it is obvious that Black has a tough time trying to hold White's attack.

Today it is considered better not to take the pawn but to play the steady d6 on move 8.

So from the position in the diagram Black plays . . .

| 8. | ... | d6 |
| 9. | Nf3 | Be6 |

Developing and attacking the white bishop on c4.

| 10. | Be6 | Re6 |
| 11. | Ng5 | |

Attacking the black rook.

| 11. | ... | Re8 |

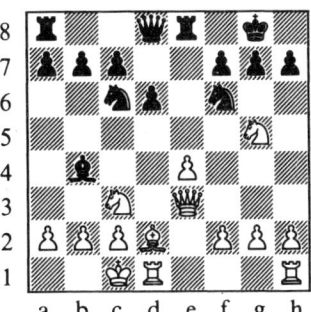

In the position in the diagram Black has a slight advantage in a complicated position. This is because his pieces are on better squares. White's queen is on the same file as Black's rook and White's bishop is hemmed in by his own pieces.

Both sides have developed their pieces in the centre but White was forced to lose time when his queen was attacked by Black's knight. So be careful to avoid placing your queen on squares in the centre where it can be attacked.

107

THE SCOTCH GAME

This opening is called the Scotch Game because Scottish players were the first to use it successfully.

The opening moves are:

WHITE	BLACK
1. e4	e5
2. Nf3	

A good move which develops a piece and attacks Black's king's pawn.

2. ...	Nc6
3. d4	

After d4 we are in the Scotch Game. With d4 White threatens to win Black's e-pawn with de5. See the diagram.

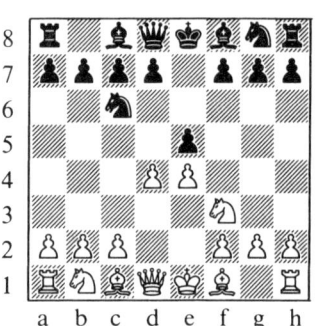

3. ...	ed4

If Black doesn't take he has problems.

If 3. ... d6 4. de5 de5 5. Qd8 ch Kd8 6. Bc4 White is ahead in development and Black cannot castle.

If 3. ... f6 4. Bc4 White is ahead in development and Black will find it difficult to castle because White's bishop on c4 controls the a2-g8 diagonal.

If 3. ... Nf6 4. de5 Ne4 then 5. Bc4 threatens Qd5 with a double attack. The queen is then threatening Qf7 mate and also Qe4.

So Black must play 3. ... ed4.

4. Nd4	

If Black now played 4. ... Nd4 then 5. Qd4 would leave the queen well placed in the centre. The difference between this position of the queen and the one looked at in the Centre Game is that the queen there could be driven away by a knight. In this position the queen cannot easily be driven away.

4.   ...   Nf6

Attacking the king's pawn.

5.   Nc3

Defending the pawn. We have now reached the position in the diagram.

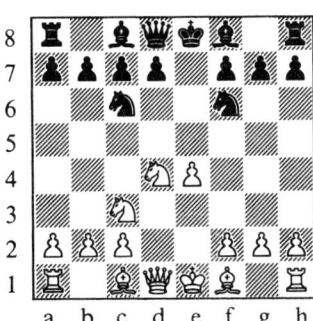

5.   ...   Bb4

Pinning the queen's knight to the king and threatening to win a pawn on the next move with Ne4. Notice that the pinned knight is powerless to defend his e-pawn. White would now like to defend his e-pawn by playing Bd3 but then Black could win the knight on d4 with Nd4. So White first plays . . .

6.   Nc6

Which pawn should Black recapture with? If 6. ... dc6 7. Qd8 ch Kd8 and Black's king is stranded in the centre.

So Black wisely plays . . .

6.   ...   bc6

7.   Bd3

Developing his bishop, guarding the e-pawn and preparing to castle.

7.   ...   d5

Hitting the e-pawn again and allowing his queen's bishop to move along the c8-h3 diagonal. Notice that Black has played to the plan of attacking the king's pawn with his last three moves.

See the diagrammed position.

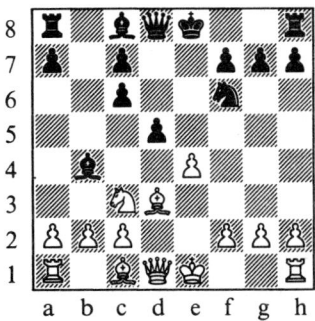

8.   ed5

White decides to get rid of the troublesome attack on his king's pawn by exchanging it for Black's d-pawn.

His bishop on d3 now has an open line, d3-h7, on which to attack the black king if he castles kingside, and he has opened up the e-file for his own rooks.

8.   ...   cd5

9.   O-O   O-O

Both sides castle immediately to get their king to safety and to bring their rooks into action along the open e-file.

10.   Bg5

Pinning the black knight to the black queen and threatening to win Black's d-pawn on the next move: 11. Bf6 Qf6 12. Nd5; or 11. Bf6 gf6 12. Nd5 and Black would not be able to play Qd5 because of Bh7 ch winning Black's queen.

10.   ...   c6

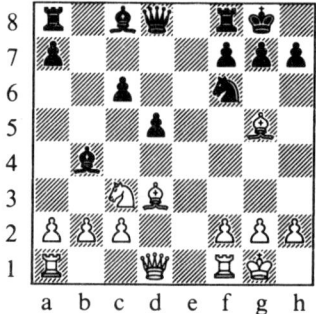

Guarding the d-pawn.

This position is equal, with chances for both sides – see the diagram.

Having played through the two games in this chapter you will now have a good idea of how to play the opening part of the game in a sensible way.

Here are two more tips:

Remember to develop quickly and, whenever possible, with threats.

Try to control the centre squares.

110

You will find that if you play the opening well you will give yourself good winning chances.

You are now off to a sound start but you will find as you get better that there is much more to learn. In Chapter 21 there is a list of books, including some on openings. Follow Spike's example and read them.

Exercise 18

(see answers in Chapter 22)

1. Which part of the board should you aim to control at the beginning of the game?

2. What should you do with your king in the opening, and why?

Chapter 19

KING AND PAWNS IN THE ENDGAME

Newcomers to chess usually find that the part of the game they enjoy most is when there are lots of pieces on the board and there are chances to play brilliant sacrifices, imaginative combinations and surprise mating attacks.

The endgame is the stage of the game least enjoyed. Usually they say that there are too few pieces to do anything interesting and so it is not worth bothering to think.

This chapter will show you that the endgame is full of ideas that surprise you and is just as interesting as any other stage of the game. There is the bonus too that if you win the endgame you will win the game itself.

For most of the game the king is forced to skulk in a corner to avoid the attacks of the enemy pieces. But once they have been swapped off and the endgame is reached the king can come out of hiding and boldly march up the board to join in the fight.

Look at this diagram.

It is White to move and his only plan is to queen the a-pawn. Can the black king catch it? Let's see.

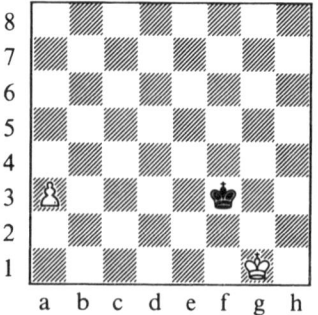

1.	a4	Ke4
2.	a5	Kd5
3.	a6	Kc6
4.	a7	Kb7

The king arrives just in time.

It was hard working out whether the black king could get back in time. So here is a rule to help you:

Draw a square using the distance from the pawn to the eighth rank as one side of the square. If the black king is inside the square with White to move then the black king can catch the pawn.

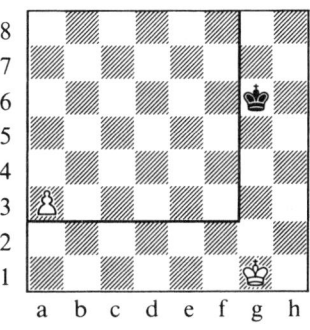

Look at this diagram and let's check to see if the rule works.

We have drawn the square and the black king is just outside. So with White to move the black king should not be able to catch the pawn.

1.	a4	Kf6
2.	a5	Ke6
3.	a6	Kd6
4.	a7	Kc6
5.	a8=Q	

Yes, the rule works, and it will save you the trouble of counting each move separately.

There is just one more thing to remember. If the pawn is on the second rank the square should be drawn from the third rank because the pawn on the second rank can move two squares forward on its first move.

The position in this diagram is important to both players. If White can queen his pawn he will win. If Black can stop him the game will be drawn.

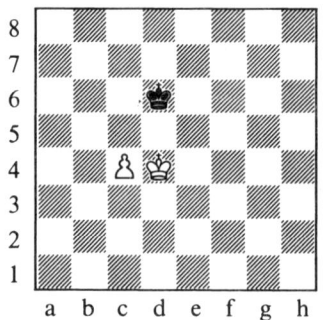

Let's see what should happen.

1.	c5 ch	Kc6
2.	Kc4	Kc7

Staying directly opposite to the white king.

3.	Kd5	Kd7
4.	c6 ch	Kc7
5.	Kc5	Kc8
6.	Kd6	Kd8
7.	c7 ch	Kc8
8.	Kc6 stalemate	

If White does not allow the stalemate he must move away from the pawn and allow it to be captured.

Here is the final position.

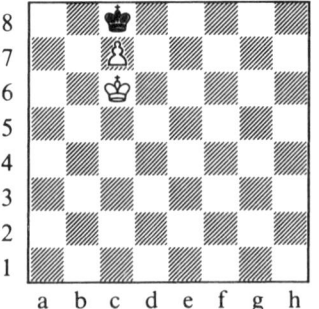

114

THE OPPOSITION

Another important position you should know about is shown in this diagram.

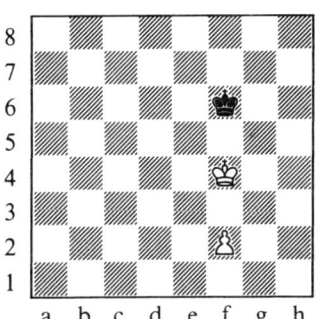

It looks very difficult for the white pawn to pass the black king and reach the queening square f8, and yet with the help of the white king it is possible.

White first advances his pawn to f3. As Black must move, his king has to move back or to the side.

1.	f3	Ke6

Black does not wish to be driven back.

2.	Kg5	Ke7

If Black plays 2. ... Ke5 he will be driven back by 3 f4 ch.

3.	Kg6	

If the white king can reach g7 it will control the queening square f8 and the black king will be powerless to stop the white pawn.

3.	...	Kf8

Stopping White's plan for the time being.

4.	f4	Kg8
5.	f5	Kf8
6.	Kf6	

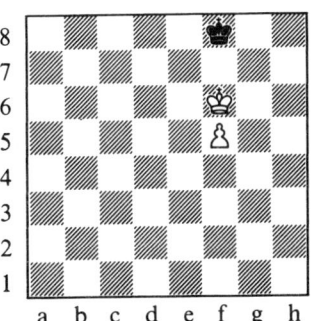

An important move which wins the game – see the position in the diagram.

Black now has only two squares available to his king, e8 and g8. He loses whichever move he plays. If 6. ... Ke8 then

7. Kg7; or if 6. ... Kg8 then 7. Ke7. In both cases the white king prevents the black king from blocking the queening square f8, and in both cases the pawn marches home in three easy moves.

If instead of playing 6. Kf6 White had played 6. f6, then Black could have drawn the game by playing 6. ... Kg8 7. f7 Kf8 8. Kf6 stalemate.

So the opposition was important for White because whatever move Black chose he was forced to move away from the queening square, allowing White to move in to control it.

Knowing about the opposition can make all the difference between winning and drawing a game when you are just one pawn ahead.

But there is one case, that of the rook's pawn, when having the opposition does not matter.

OTHER KING AND PAWN ENDINGS

Look at this diagram to find out what happens with the rook's pawn.

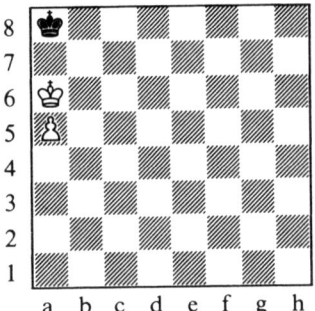

White has the opposition, so Black must move.

1.	...	Kb8
2.	Kb6	Ka8
3.	a6	Kb8
4.	a7	Ka8
5.	Ka6 stalemate	

There is no way that White can force Black out of the corner, so the game is drawn.

Even when White manages to get into the corner he cannot win.

116

In this diagram with White to play there are two lines.

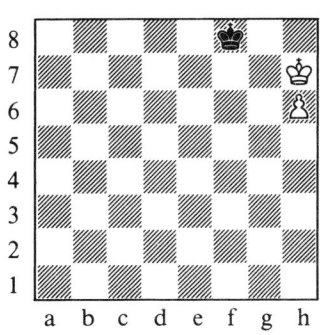

1.	Kg6	Kg8	or	1.	Kh8	Kf7
2.	h7	Kh8		2.	h7	Kf8
3.	Kh6 stalemate				stalemate	

This is the final position in the second line of play.

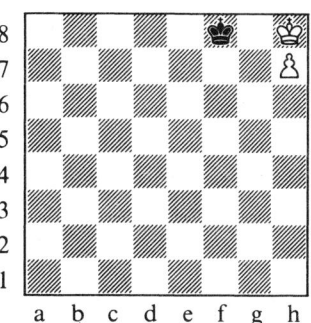

So, if in a king and pawn ending you can choose which pawn to have, don't pick the rook's pawn if the enemy king can reach the queening square.

This position looks about level as both players have two pawns.

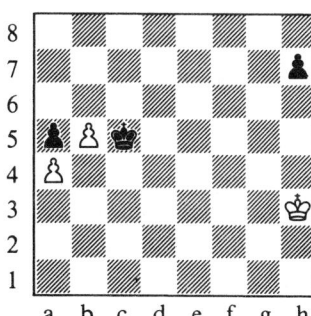

In fact White is winning easily. Let's take a look at the play.

If 1. ... Kb4, intending to capture the a-pawn, then 2. b6 Ka4 3. b7 and the pawn queens, or if 1. ... Kd6 then 2. Kh4 Ke6 (the king comes over to protect the h-pawn) 3. Kh5 Kf6 4. b6 and the pawn queens.

If Black does nothing and just waits White will first capture the h-pawn and then take his king over to the queenside. He will force Black's king to move away from his pawn on a5 and will capture it. With two united passed pawns the win will be easy.

This diagram shows a position to remember. It can happen in any part of the board.

Whoever has the move loses. Why? Because he is forced to move away from defending his own pawn.

White to move: 1. Kd4 Kb4 and wins.

Black to move: 1. ... Kb3 2. Kb5 and wins.

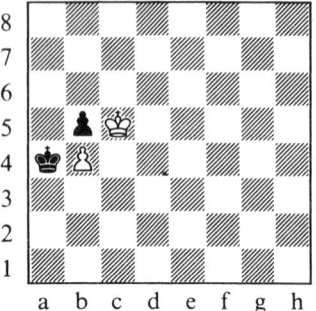

In this diagram it looks as if Black must win.

He is just one square away from queening his pawn and his king is ready to stop the white pawns from queening.

But, as so often in chess, the unexpected happens.

1.   Ke6   d8=Q

2.   f7 mate

So, although a queen down, White won.

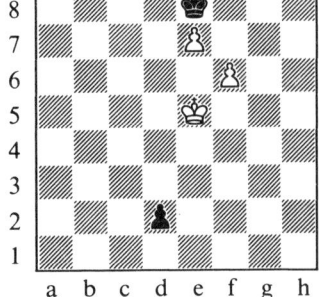

This is the final position.

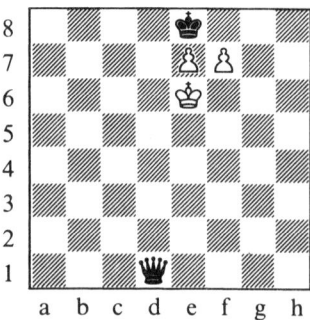

118

Exercise 19

(see answers in Chapter 22)

Say what the result will be in each of the following positions. It is Black to move each time.

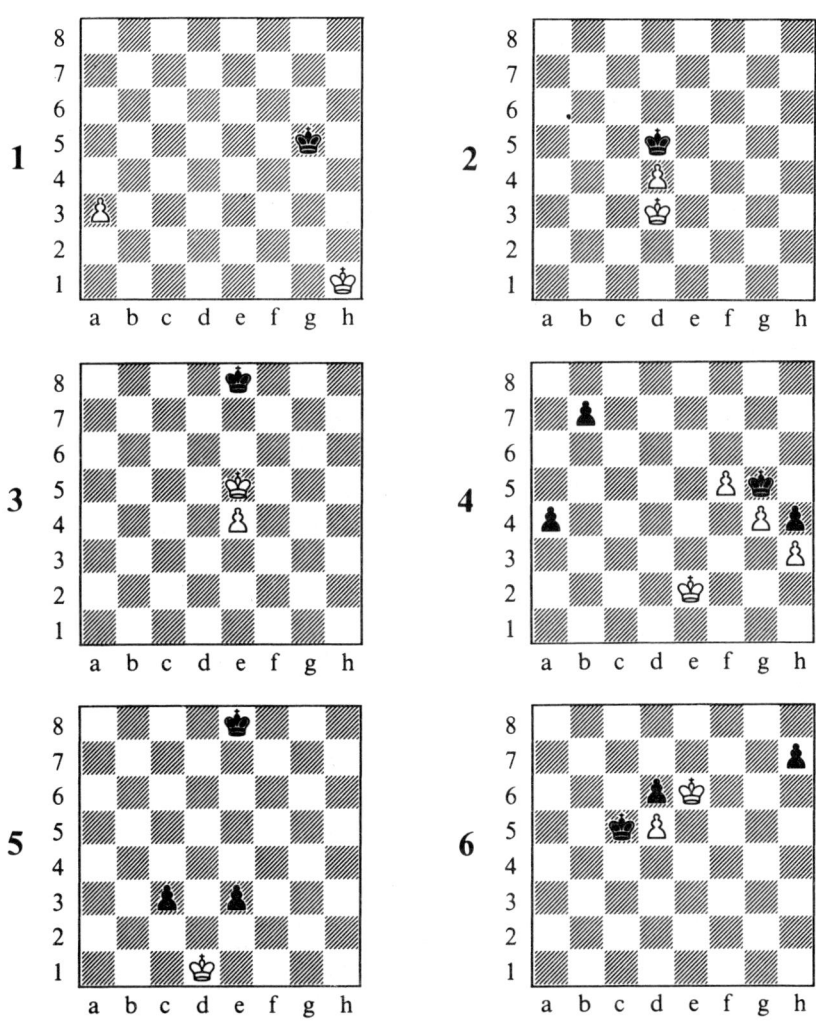

Chapter 20

SOME FRIENDS OF SPIKE

Jonathan Walton

Jonathan usually meets Spike and his friends with a beaming smile and this cheers everybody up.

His mother, Joan, taught him the moves when he was only six and he showed immediate interest. He played regularly with his dad Steve who quickly noticed his natural talent and did all he could to help him to develop it. When only seven he played his first tournament at the Preston Easter Schools Congress and won his event with a remarkable score of 20 out of 20!

At the local chess club he was soon making his mark by his obvious aptitude for the game. Leading local players Brett Lund and George Ellison were very impressed and did all that they could to advise and encourage Jonathan.

For a seven-year-old his results in local competitions were exceptional and included one first and two second places in tournaments for twelve-year-olds! These performances earned him a regular place in the Lancashire county junior team where he played very well. He was equally success-ful against adult players, scoring 60 per cent for Preston Chess Club in the local league when only eight.

In May 1986 he gained national recog-nition by coming second at the Lloyds

Bank BCF Squad Tournament. This was followed in the summer by third place in the British Championship Under 9 event with a grading prize for the best under 8.

Jonathan continues to score well in local adult tournaments. For example, a week before his tenth birthday he won the Bolton Minor Quickplay with 5½/6.

From this description you might well imagine that Jonathan does little else but play chess. This is far from the case. He is a friendly and enthusiastic cub-scout, a keen member of the Church Lads Brigade and swims well for his age. Jonathan likes to do his very best at anything he tries and this is shown in the high standard of his school work. He also loves to play football, pool and to join in improvised games both with his pals at school and his bright younger sister Katie at home.

Spike thinks it is highly likely that Jonathan will become a top class player. From what you have heard so far you'll probably agree.

Jonathan played the following interesting game in the Bolton Easter Minor Tournament 1987.

WHITE	*BLACK*
D. Wallwork	**J. S. Walton**
1. **e4**	**e6**
2. **d4**	**d5**
3. **ed5**	**ed5**

This opening is called the Exchange Variation of the French Defence and this position is considered to be level.

4.	Bd3	Nf6
5.	h3	h6
6.	Bf4	c5 !

An aggressive move attacking White's centre pawn.

7.	c3	Nc6
8.	Nf3	cd4
9.	Nd4	Bc5

Both players have now developed in sound fashion.

10.	Nb5	

With the threat of Nc7 ch forking king and rook.

10.	...	0-0
11.	0-0	a6
12.	Nb5a3	

If instead the tempting Nc7 then Ra7 and the knight is trapped.

12.	...	Re8

Wisely posting his rook on the open file.

13.	Nd2	b5
14.	Nc2	d4 !
15.	Qf3	Bb7
16.	Ne4	Ne4

If White had played instead 16. cd4 then 16. ... Nd4 17. Qb7 Ra7 18. Qb8 Qd7 and White's queen would have been lost – a deep and cunning trap.

17.	Be4	Rc8
18.	Radl	Qf6
19.	cd4	Nd4!!
20.	Rd4	

Position after 6. ... c5!

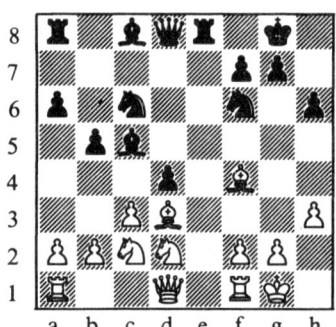

Position after 14. ... d4!

Position after 19. ... Nd4!!

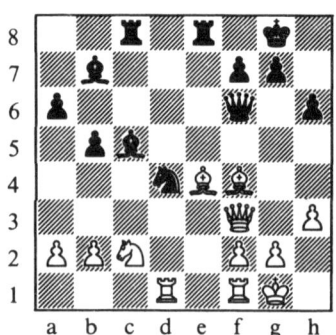

122

White plays the best move but is still losing.

20.	...	Bd4
21.	Bb7	Rc2
22.	Bc1	Qf3

Jonathan shows a deep understanding of the position. Swapping off queens and going into an endgame will make his win easier because he has extra material.

23.	Bf3	Bf2!
24.	Rf2	Re1 ch
25.	Kh2?	

Not best. 25. Rf1 Rf1ch 26. Kf1 Rc1ch would have been better but still losing.

25.	...	Rf2
26.	Resigns	

A wise decision as the bishops are no match for the rooks. For example 26. Bf4 Rf3 27. gf3 Re2 ch 28. Kg3 Rb2 and Black will soon queen his extra pawn on the queenside.

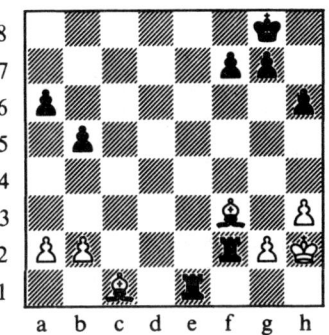

The final position

Nicola Romer

Another friend of Spike's is an amiable teenager called Nicola who has a quiet sense of humour and a tenacious approach to all she does, including chess.

She is a talented all-rounder with many interests. In addition to being a very good chess player for her age, she plays the piano and violin well and is a keen dancer with medals and certificates in ballet, tap and modern dancing. To find time to enjoy all these hobbies at a high standard and perform well in school is quite remarkable.

Nicola's father taught her the moves when she was eight and was her main opponent until she joined an enthusiastic chess club at her primary school. She soon became a member of a successful school team which more than once won the District Primary School Championship. For a short time – between the age of nine and ten – Nicola's other interests assumed greater importance than chess, but the emergence of her younger brother James as one of the best players of his age in the area rekindled a keen interest in chess. He continued to provide Nicola with plenty of opposition by winning the Lancashire Schools Under 9 Championship, the District Schools Championship for a record three years and representing Lancashire each year since the age of nine. Their friendly rivalry has helped both to develop their chess.

It was, however, when Nicola joined the highly successful club at Poulton-le-Fylde, at the age of eleven, that her game began to flourish. Her flair was soon noticed and she received encouragement and help from adult members. She won the Poulton Club Junior Championship in 1987 against stern opposition from several of the best boys in the district and went on to represent the club regularly in the local league. County honours followed and recently she held her own as a member of the Lancashire Under 14 team in the National Youth Championships. She has now started to play in tournaments and is rapidly making her mark: her best result to date being second prize in the Lancashire Junior Under 18 Congress at the age of fourteen – a performance which made the boys in the county sit up and take notice, especially those she beat!

Nicola has found that it isn't easy being a girl in a chess scene where nearly all the players are boys. At the school chess club, several of the boys avoid playing her in case she beats them – Spike thinks it is time they grew up. Membership of the British Women's Chess Federation has made Nicola realise that other girls in school chess clubs meet this problem too. In Nicola's case she has outsmarted them by becoming established as the club coach!

This position was reached in a game played in the 1986 Blackpool Chess Congress. H.B.Scott was White and Nicola was Black. Nicola has achieved a won position. She is a pawn up and her opponent's knight is pinned, so that if it moves, Black's bishop on g7 will capture White's rook on a1. However, in spite of these advantages it looks as though the game will continue for many more moves. See how Nicola wraps up the game in only seven more moves by attacking along the weak black squares around Black's king.

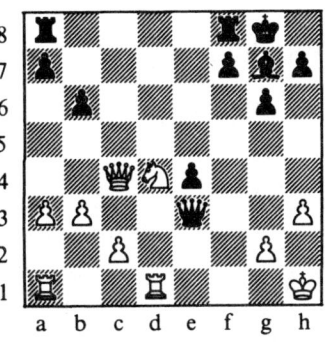

1.	...	b5!

A clever decoy pawn sacrifice which wins material however White plays. If 2. Qb5 Bd4 wins the knight. If 2. Nb5 Ba1 3. Ra1 Ra8c8 and White loses his pawn on c2.

2.	Qd5	Ra8d8
3.	Qb5	Bd4
4.	Re1	Qf4
5.	Ra1d1	Be5

Setting up a mating pattern on the black squares.

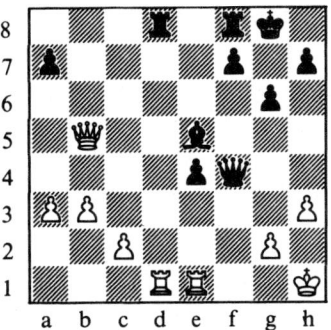

Position after 5. ... Be5

6.   Kg1   e3!

Black now threatens to finish the game with 7. ... Qf2 ch 8. Kh1 Rd2. If White then plays 9. Rd2 Black mates with 9. ... Qe1 ch 10. Qf1 Qf1 mate or 9. Rg1 Qg3 with mate on h2 or the loss of White's queen by 10. Qe5 Qe5. After 6. ... e3 White cannot defend himself and is completely lost.

7.   Rd8

A blunder but every other move loses so it didn't really matter.

7.   ...   Qf2 ch

8.   Resigns

His only move was 8. Kh1 when 8. ... Qe1 ch 9. Qf1 Qf1 was mate.

A powerful and pleasing finish by Nicola.

The final position

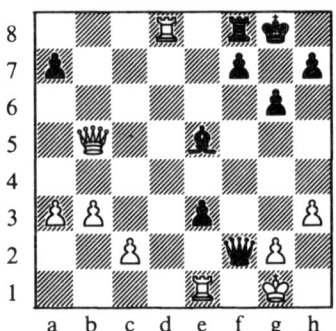

Darryl Wolstencroft

Yet another good friend of Spike's is Darryl, who is a quiet, earnest, unassuming young teenager with real talent for chess and remarkable dedication to playing it well. He was taught to play at the age of five by his brother, Gary, and was soon winning more games than he lost.

Each week, Darryl plays at two chess clubs, representing Bispham in the local league and Poulton-le-Fylde in the Lancashire Clubs competition. He also plays regularly in most of the tournaments in the North-West and several much further afield. He is fortunate to have an equally dedicated mum and dad, Marlene and Trevor, who ferry him all over the place, and take great interest and pride in his achievements.

You will see from the following description that he has already a most impressive record and Spike thinks that he has a good chance of becoming a full international player in the not too distant future. At ten, he was selected to play in the Lancashire Under 11 team and over the next two years maintained a 100 per cent record. In the same period, he won the Under 10 prize in the British Under 11 Championship at Brighton. These results led to his selection for the England Under 11 team in matches against Scotland and Wales. On both occasions he won every game.

Also at the age of eleven, he beat George Ellison, the Blackpool and Fylde League champion and at thirteen capped this result by beating Brett Lund, the Lancashire champion. Already, at the age of eleven, he was regularly winning prizes in Minor events at adult tournaments and has now moved up to play in Major events where he continues to impress. He now plays to a national grade of about 160 which places him among the top juniors in the country.

Darryl has an excellent temperament for chess and seems able – like all the top players – to produce his best form when it really matters.

He is also a keen all-round sportsman who enjoys playing football and tennis with his friends and a regular round of golf with his dad at weekends. He is an enthusiastic supporter of Liverpool Football Club and a fan of his local team, Blackpool, whose matches he regularly attends.

Darryl played the following scintillating game in his first match for the Lancashire County First Team.

WHITE	BLACK
D. Wolstencroft	**F. K. Kneale**

1.	e4	c5
2.	c3	

With the idea of playing 3. d4 to establish a good pawn centre with pawns on e4 and d4.

2.	...	Nc6
3.	d4	cd4
4.	cd4	

White now has a good pawn centre.

4.	...	d5
5.	e5	

The best move, maintaining his pawn centre and stopping Black's knight from going to f6.

5.	...	Bf5
6.	Bd3	Bd3
7.	Qd3	e6
8.	Nf3	Bb4 ch
9.	Nc3	Nf8e7
10.	0-0	0-0
11.	a3	Ba5
12.	Ng5	g6

Forced to prevent mate on h7.

13.	g4!	

An imaginative move played in order to prevent ... h5 by Black. White is intending to play Qh3 as his next move threatening mate on h7 and with a pawn on g4 would be able to meet ... h5 with gh5.

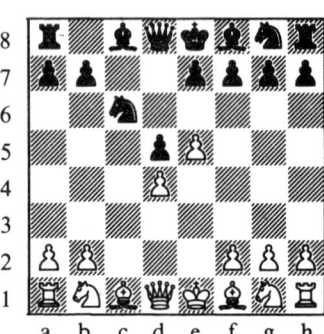

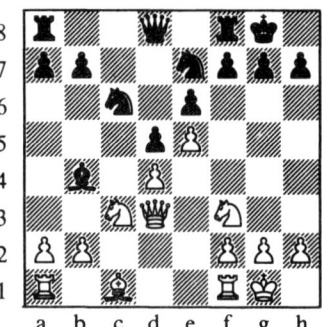

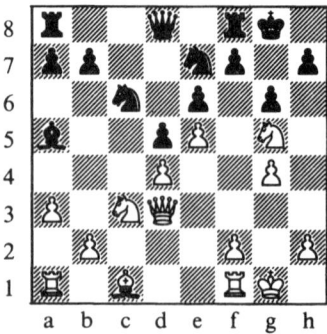

128

13.	...	h6
14.	Nh3	

This is best. Darryl now switches his plan and decides to advance his f-pawn in order to bring his king's rook into the attack.

14.	...	g5?
15.	f4!	

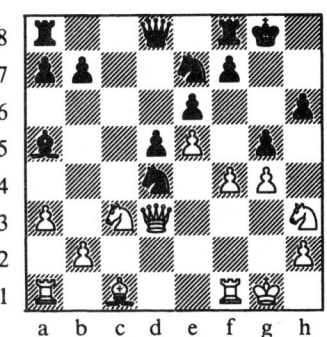

Position after 15. ... Nd4!

Hitting the weak g-pawn which is now attacked three times.

15.	...	Nd4!

A good try to get back into the game. He is hoping for Qd4 when ... Bb6 would win White's queen.

16.	fg5	

Darryl wisely ignores this capture and carries on demolishing Black's kingside.

16.	...	Nd4c6
17.	gh6	Ng6?
18.	h7ch!	Kh7
19.	Ng5ch	Kg7

If 19. ... Kg8 then 20 Qh3 with either mate on h7 or the win of Black's queen.

20.	Rf7ch!!	

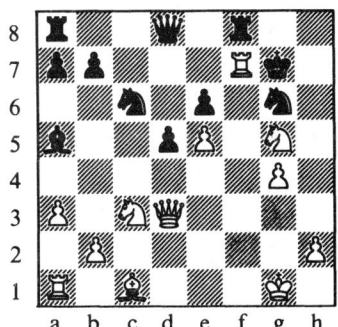

Position after 20. Rf7ch!!

A lovely move and a bolt from the blue for Black. If 20. ... Rf7 then 21. Ne6ch wins Black's queen.

20.	...	Kg8
21.	Qg6ch	Resigns

Black decides he has had enough as Darryl has three different ways of checkmating. Can you find them?

Chapter 21

HOW TO BECOME A BETTER PLAYER

It is tempting to move fast to show your opponent what a brilliant player you are and how quickly you can think out the best moves. DON'T – move slowly, take your time, and think carefully before you move.

When you have decided which move you want to play, check carefully to make sure that you haven't missed anything. Tony Miles, formerly England's No 1 grandmaster and now one of the United States' leading players, always writes down the move he has decided upon, puts down his pen and checks to make sure he has made the right move. Only when he is absolutely sure does he then play the move. Follow Tony's example.

When you have found a good move to play, don't be satisfied. Have another look at the position to see if there is an even better one.

Try to play to your best standard at all times. Some junior players waste a lot of time playing without bothering to think. If you obey this rule you will quickly improve your game.

Try not to get rattled if you make a mistake and lose a piece. Keep on thinking and trying – your opponent may become overconfident and make an even worse error. In chess the player who makes the *last* mistake loses the game.

After the game is finished, try to find time to play through it with your opponent, discussing what you both thought about the positions of the game. In this way you will both learn a lot.

When you have a friend who is about your own standard, it is tempting to spend all your time playing with him. DON'T – try to play with as many different people as possible. Each player has a different way of playing and you will learn many more ideas by seeing how different opponents meet your ideas.

Spend as much time as you can practising the game. "Practice makes perfect" is as true in chess as in any other sport.

If you are lucky enough to attend a school where chess is played then join the school chess club and play as often as possible. Sign up to play in the school competitions and try hard to get into the school team. Find out where there is a local chess club and join it. This will put you in touch with good adult players and strong junior players from other schools. When only eight years old, Nigel Short, England's strongest ever junior player, was playing for Bolton Chess Club in the Manchester and District Chess League.

If there are several chess clubs in your area find out if any of them run a junior coaching scheme. Join the club that runs a scheme and you will get free regular coaching by the best players in the club.

It is a good idea to read a chess magazine regularly. There are two main magazines, both of them good. They are **PERGAMON CHESS**, Railway Road, Sutton Coldfield, West Midlands B73 6AZ, which comes out monthly at a price of £1.75 per copy or £17.50 per annum for 17 issues, and the **BRITISH CHESS MAGAZINE**, 9 Market Street, St Leonards-on-Sea, East Sussex TN38 0DQ, which is also monthly and costs £18.00 per year or £1.50 per copy.

Both magazines are packed with up-to-date news on the current chess scene, with interesting games, problems, book reviews, advertisements for chess-playing computers, chess tournaments and other events.

It is a good idea to take a copy of each before deciding which one you enjoy reading most.

As you become a better player you will want to read more about the game. Here are a few suggestions.

For your opening play you can do no better than turn to **CHESS OPENINGS FOR JUNIORS** by J.N.Walker, published by Oxford University Press. You will enjoy the simple and direct way in which the author discusses several openings and your knowledge of opening ideas will increase considerably.

To improve your middle game play you should read **HOW TO PLAY THE MIDDLE GAME IN CHESS** by John Littlewood, published by Batsford.

This is a most interesting book which will help you to think clearly and to plan ahead once the opening moves have been played.

The most useful endgame book is undoubtedly Paul Keres's **PRACTICAL CHESS ENDINGS**, again published by Batsford. All the basic positions are discussed and illustrated by examples from master play. Careful reading of this book should rapidly improve your endgame play.

You can either buy these books directly from a bookshop or book supplier – listed below – or ask your library to obtain them for you. Most libraries are most obliging in meeting requests.

The following book suppliers will be only too pleased to meet your orders for books.

ManCHESSter Supplies, 6 Thetford Road, Great Sankey, Warrington, Cheshire WA5 3EQ.

Pergamon Chess, Railway Road, Sutton Coldfield, West Midlands BA73 6AZ.

The British Chess Magazine Limited, 9 Market Street, St Leonards-on-Sea, East Sussex TN38 0DQ.

Brian Eley, Dearne Road, Bolton-on-Dearne, Rotherham S63 8JR.

If you are interested in chess computers, several suppliers will be pleased to give you information and supply their computers:

Doska Chess Supplies, 16 Carleton Gardens, Poulton-le-Fylde, Lancs FY2 7PB. Telephone: 0253 899742. Proprietor Ken Gorman sells all the leading makes and will give you an independent view of their respective merits.

Competence, The Chess Computer Specialists, 26 Eversholt Street, London

NW1 1BA. Their magazine CHESS COMPUTER NEWS provides up-to-date information on the chess computer scene.

Countrywise Computers, Victoria House, 1 High Street, Wilburton, Cambridgeshire CB6 3RB. Telephone 0353 740323. This firm sells the whole range of computers and will provide detailed comparability charts on request.

Finally, when you have been playing for a short while, say about six months, you'll find it fun to enter one of the many weekend congresses. You may say, "Not likely, I'm not good enough yet, those experts will wipe the floor with me." Don't worry, there are sections for juniors of every age and also a novice section for people who have not been playing very long.

In a weekend congress you'll play five or six games against people about your own standard. The tournament is arranged so that winners of games play other winners and losers other losers. So it is likely that you'll win some games and lose others, but what is certain is that you'll have a whale of a time.

Good luck!

Chapter 22

ANSWERS TO EXERCISES

Exercise 1

1. There should be a white square by each player's right hand, as in the diagram.

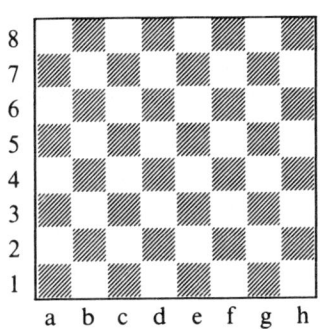

2. Rook or castle, knight, bishop, queen, king, pawn (in any order).

3. See the diagram. Make sure that you have placed the white queen on a white square and the black queen on a black square.

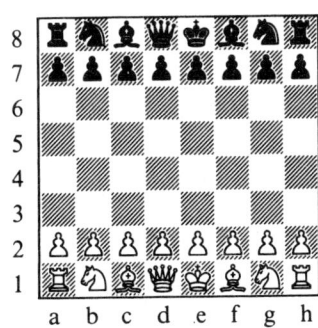

4. The squares with a cross are d6, e4 and h1.

Exercise 2

1. From b1, providing that there is nothing in the way, the rook can travel to b2, b3, b4, b5, b6, b7, b8 and a1, c1, d1, e1, f1, g1 and h1.

2. A rook on e5 could capture pieces anywhere along the e-file and anywhere along the fifth rank.

    So if your pieces are on any four of these squares you are right: a5, b5, c5, d5, f5, g5, h5 and e1, e2, e3, e4, e6, e7 and e8.

3. The knight on e8, because its own pawn is in the way. Rooks cannot jump over their own or enemy pieces.

Exercise 3

1. Your pawns should be placed on e7, f6 and h6.

2. Your pawns should be placed on d7, f7, c6, g6, c4, g4, d3 and f3.

3. The rook on c3, the bishop on d2 and the rook on d6.

Exercise 4

1.

a) From d8 the queen can go anywhere along the a8-h8 rank, the d-file from d7-d1, the diagonal from c7-a5 and the diagonal from e7-h4. See the diagram.

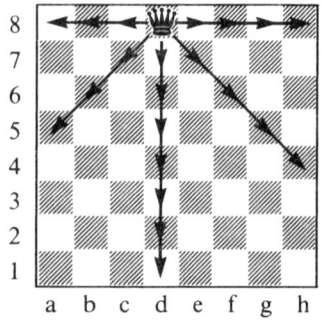

b) From e5 the queen can travel anywhere along the e-file, the fifth rank and the diagonals h2-b8 and a1-h8. See the diagram.

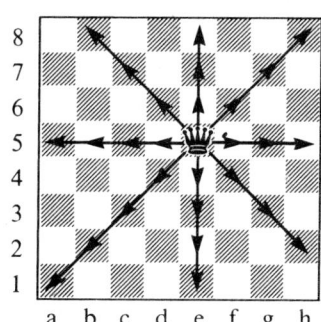

2. The queen on b3, the pawn on d5 and the bishop on f7.

Exercise 5

1. The bishop on c1 can go anywhere along the d2-h6 diagonal and to b2. It cannot go to a3 because that square is occupied by its own pawn.

2. The bishop on f5 can go anywhere along the diagonals b1-h7 and h3-c8.

3. The black pawn on a2, the black rook on g2, the black pawn on e6 and the black bishop on a8.

Exercise 6

A king on c6 can go to b7, c7, d7, d6, d5, c5, b5 and b6.

Exercise 7

1. The pawns on a4 and e3.

2. They can move to a5 and e4.

3. The pawn on e3 can capture the enemy bishop.

4. It will capture on f4 and remain on that square until it is moved forward later in the game to f5.

5. The pawn on c4 cannot move because the enemy pawn on c5 is in the way.

Exercise 8

1. The king can either take the pawn on g2 or move to h2.

2. The king can either move out of check to any of the squares e1, e2, f2, g2, g1, or the white knight on f3 can capture the black knight on d2.

3. The king can move out of check to the squares c1, d2, e1, e2.
   The rook on h4 can capture the bishop.
   The white bishop on b1 can move to c2, between the black bishop and the white king.

4. The king can move away from the h-file to g2.
   The knight can play to h3, between the rook and the king.
   The white queen can capture the rook.

Exercise 9

1. Not checkmate. The king can move to h7.

2. Checkmate.

3. Checkmate.

4. Not checkmate. The king can move to g7.

5. Not checkmate. The black queen can capture the pawn on f7.

6. Checkmate.

Exercise 10

1. Black cannot castle on the queenside because he has already moved his queen's rook.
   He cannot castle on the kingside as his knight is in the way.

2. Black can castle on either side of the board.

3. Black can castle on the kingside but not on the queenside, where he would be moving into check by the bishop.

4. Black cannot castle as he is in check.

5. Black cannot castle on the kingside as his bishop on f8 is in the way.
   He cannot castle on the queenside as he would be moving into check by the bishop.

6. Black can castle on the queenside (it does not matter that his rook is threatened).

Exercise 11

Well done if you managed to play through this game and reach the position in the diagram. You can now score your own game successfully and read chess books.

Exercise 12

1. Position **B** is stalemate.

2. Position **A** is not stalemate. White can play his pawn to b4. Stalemate can only occur when the king is not in check and there is nó other move with any of the pieces or pawns.

3. 1. Qd4 Kb5 2. Kd6 Ka4 3. Qb2 Ka5 4. Kc5 Ka4 5. Qb4 mate
    or
    1. Qd4 Kb7 2. Kd6 Ka6 3. Qb4 Ka7 4. Kc7 Ka6 5. Qb6 mate.
    There are other possibilities besides these.

4. 1. ... Qg3 ch! 2. Qg3 stalemate (forced or the white queen is lost). White, two pawns up and both about to queen, was really sick at only drawing this game.

Exercise 13

1. 1. Kb6 Kf1 2. Kc5 Kg1 3. Ra2 Kf1 4. Kd4 Ke1 5. Kd3 Kf1 6. Ke3 Kg1 7. Kf3 Kh1 8. Kg3 Kg1 9. Ra1 mate.

2. 1. Rc8 Kb3 2. Kd4 Kb2 3. Kd3 Kb1 4. Kd2 Kb2 5. Rb8 ch Ka3 6. Kc2 Ka4

7. Kc3 Ka5 8. Kc4 Ka6 9. Kc5 Ka7
10. Rb1 Ka6 11. Rb2 (the waiting
move) 11. ... Ka7 12. Kc6 Ka8 13. Kc7
Ka7 14. Ra2 mate.

I hope that this chapter has made you
feel that the endgame is interesting
and worth spending time on. Learning
to play it well will give you many
extra wins.

Exercise 14

1. Ne5 was a mistake. Black plays
   Qa5 ch winning the knight on e5 on
   his next move.

2. Black plays Nc2 checking the king
   and attacking the rook. After the
   king has moved he simply captures
   the rook with his knight.

3. After Bd5 Black must lose a knight.

4. Qg6 – the queen cannot be taken
   because the white bishop on b3 is
   pinning the pawn on f7 to the black
   king.

Exercise 15

1. No. If 1. ... Qe2 then 2. Ra1e1 and
   Black either loses his queen or allows
   the back row mate.

2. If you managed this one you did very
   well.
   1. Rh8 Rb7 2. Rh7 ch Ke6 3. Rb7.
   If after 1. Rh8 Black plays 1. ... Kg7
   then 2. b8=Q and the white queen

and white rook are guarding each other, so Black must lose.

3. Yes. White plays 1. Nc6 giving discovered check from the white queen on e2. If 1. ... Be7 then 2. Nd8.

4. 1. Rg3 giving discovered check by the bishop on b2. If 1. ... Qf6 then 2. Bf6 mate.

5. Rg8 double discovered check. Both the bishop on b2 and the rook on g8 are checking the black king. It cannot move out of check by capturing the white rook on g8 as it is covered by the other white rook on g1. Rf8g8 by Black is not possible as the bishop on b2 would still be checking the king.

6. 1. Nf6 or 1. Nh6 double discovered checkmate. 1. ... Bg7 is not possible as the knight would still be checking the king.

Exercise 16

1. 1. Qf8 ch Rf8 2. Rh6 ch Kd7 3. Ra6 wins a piece.

2. 1. ... Qg2 ch 2. Qg2 Rd1 mate.

3. 1. Qf8 ch Kf8 2. Rh8 mate.

4. 1. Bh7 ch Kh7 2. Qh5 ch Kg8 3. Ng5 Re8 4. Qf7 ch Kh8 5. Rh3 mate.

   If 1. ... Kh8 then 2. Qh5 g6 3. Bg6 ch Kg7 4. Qh7 mate.

5. 1. ... Qh1 ch 2. Kh1 Nf2 ch 3. Kg2 Ng4 wins the queen, leaving Black a piece up.

6.   1. Qa5 ch Ka5 2. Ra7 mate.

Exercise 17

1.   1. Rd6 Rd6 2. Re8 mate.
     If after 1. Rd6 Black does not capture
     he will be a rook down and will
     lose.

2.   1. ... Qa1 ch 2. Qf1 Rd1 wins the
     queen and the game.

3.   1. Qh6 ch Kg8 2. Nf6 mate.

4.   1. Ne7 ch Kh8 2. Qh7 ch Kh7 3. Rh3
     mate.

5.   1. Re6 Qe6 2. Qg3 ch Kh8 3. Qg7
     mate.

6.   1. Qh3 Rd8 2. Qh7 ch Kf8 3. Qh8
     mate.

7.   1. Bh6 gh6 2. Qh6 Rf8d8 3. Qh8 mate
     or
     1. Bh6 Qc5 2. Bg5 Qg5 3. Qh8 mate.

8.   1. ... Nh3 ch 2. gh3 Rg2 ch 3. Kh1
     Rh2 ch 4. Kg1 Rc2g2 mate
     or
     1. ... Nh3 ch 2. Kh1 Rg2 3. Rf1e1 Rh2
     mate.

Exercise 18

1.   The centre.

2.   You should castle. The king will
     then be safe, and a rook will also
     have been brought into play.

Exercise 19

1. Black just moves inside the square in time. 1. ... Kf6 2. a4 Ke6 3. a5 Kd6 4. a6 Kc6 5. a7 Kb7 catching the pawn.

2. Black draws. 1. ... Kd6 2. Ke4 Ke6 3. d5 ch Kd6 4. Kd4 Kd7 5. Kc5 Kc7 6. d6 ch Kd7 7. Kd5 Kd8 8. Ke6 Ke8 9. d7 ch Kd8 10. Kd6 stalemate.

3. Black draws. 1. ... Ke7 2. Kf5 Kf7 3. e5 Ke7 4. e6 Ke8 5. Kf6 Kf8 6. e7 ch Ke8 7. Ke6 stalemate.

4. White draws. He has time to take his king to stop Black's pawns. 1. Kd2 b5 2. Kc3 Kf6 draw. Neither side can capture a pawn without losing the game. If, for example, 3. Kb4 Kg5 4. Kb5 then 4. ... a3 and the pawn queens. If Black's king moves to f4 then White plays f6 and queens the pawn.

5. Black wins by moving his king anywhere, say 1. ... Ke7. White is then forced to move and therefore cannot stop one of the pawns from queening. If 2. Kc2 or 2. Kc1 then 2. ... e2 and the e-pawn queens next move. If 2. Ke2 or 2. Ke1 then 2. ... c2 and the c-pawn queens.

6. Black wins. After 1. ... h5 2. Kf5 Kd5 3. Kg5 Ke4 4. Kh4 Ke3 White's king is cut off from the queening square.